The Seven Stages of an Enlightened Teacher

Second Edition

The Seven Stages of an Enlightened Teacher

Second Edition

Christine Jax

ROWMAN & LITTLEFIELD EDUCATION

A division of

ROWMAN & LITTLEFIELD PUBLISHERS, INC.
Lanham • New York • Toronto • Plymouth, UK

Published by Rowman & Littlefield Education
A division of Rowman & Littlefield Publishers, Inc.
A wholly owned subsidary of The Rowman & Littlefield Publishing Group, Inc.
4501 Forbes Boulevard, Suite 200, Lanham, Maryland 20706
http://www.rowmaneducation.com

Estover Road, Plymouth PL6 7PY, United Kingdom

British Library Cataloguing in Publication Information Available

Library of Congress Cataloging-in-Publication Data

Jax, Christine, 1959–
    The seven stages of an enlightened teacher / Christine Jax.—2nd ed.
        p. cm.
    Includes bibliographical references.
    ISBN 978-1-61048-074-1 (cloth : alk. paper)—ISBN 978-1-61048-075-8 (pbk. : alk.
paper)—ISBN 978-1-61048-076-5 (electronic)
    1. Teachers.   2. Teaching—Psychological aspects.   3. Education—Philosophy.
I. Title.
    LB1775.J39 2011
    371.1—dc22   2011006334

∞™ The paper used in this publication meets the minimum requirements of American
National Standard for Information Sciences—Permanence of Paper for Printed Library
Materials, ANSI/NISO Z39.48-1992.

Printed in the United States of America

To my love Jesus (Zeus) Castillo
who amazes, inspires, and blesses me every day
with his quick wit, kind heart, loving spirit,
and passion for me and life.

Contents

Acknowledgments

Thank you to my great friends for their love and support, most notably Michelle Beinner, Ann Arkell, Brenda Torre, Sandra Grigg, Elena Kays, Marianne McKenna, and Ann Licatero.

Thank you to my beautiful daughters, Marie, Ellen, and Laura Hansen, who make me proud and happy each and every day. To share a path with you amazing women is a highlight of my life.

Thank you to the teachers who reviewed and improved the manuscript: Liz Adamson, Kim Anderson, Linda Ashkin, Sheron Brown, Diana Ciesko, Tony Faaborg, Jen Funk, Natalie Mendez, Teri Stiles, and Lynn Sweeden.

Introduction

Spirituality, the Soul, and Education

> Everything is laid out for you. Your path is straight ahead of you.
> Sometimes it's invisible but it's there. You may not know where it's
> going, But you have to follow the path. It's the path of the Creator. It's
> the only path there is.

> —Chief Leon Shenandoah

After years of working with, studying, and educating teachers, it has become
apparent to me that exceptional teachers have gone through a series of stages
to arrive at their level of competence. While individual teachers may go back
and forth between stages or remain forever at a particular stage, effective
teachers operate from three specific stages of spiritual enlightenment, and the
greatest of those at the final stage—a stage of inspirational mastery.

When I first realized how teachers develop and express this development
through their teaching, I thought I was looking at psychological stages. While
many of the attributes I saw certainly are grounded in psychological aspects
of the personality, I soon realized that there was something else. There was
something more that happened over time to the amazing teacher—something
to her perception of self, relationships with others, and connection to the
sacred.

As I sought to discover what this added dimension was, I turned to
education research and the writings of education scholars. Before long,
however, I found myself relating the words and actions of these teachers to
religious scholars and mystics. That is when it hit me. There is a significant
spiritual aspect to teaching, and great teachers develop through a series of
Seven Stages—spiritual stages that encompass personality and incorporate
pedagogy.

1

I decided to dedicate time and effort to the understanding of these spiritual stages so I could share them with teachers who were committed to personal growth and improved teaching.

This book is a result of this journey, and it is dedicated with admiration to our teachers, especially those who see teaching as a profession, learning as life-long, and the intersection of the two as transformational.

HOW TO USE THIS BOOK

As a teacher, you can use this book in three ways. First, you can employ it to assess at which Stage you currently are operating. You likely will see aspects of yourself in a couple of Stages. It is through this analysis that you will identify your strengths and deficits and determine which areas of your life need your attention. This will help you bring yourself consistently to the highest level at which you can operate at this time.

Second, by clearly articulating what a teacher at a higher level looks like, the book provides a road map for how to gauge and advance your competency as a master teacher in the true sense of the word master.

Third, if you mentor or instruct other teachers, you can use this book to further develop your knowledge base and coaching skills.

Regardless of what Stage you may think you are at, read each Stage. The attributes of the Stages are cumulative, so learning the concepts at each Stage helps you understand yourself. Do the prayers, mediations, and journaling for each Stage as well, as they can inspire and motivate you even if you are not at that particular Stage. Also, familiarize yourself with the teaching strategies too. Everyone can get into a rut, and you might be surprised at what parts of yourself have not developed as thoroughly as they can.

As teachers, we often get caught up too easily in the details of getting through the day and forget the true meaning of being called to the profession. This book improves our teaching because it reminds us that teaching is for a special few. But, it also explores our humanity and the commonalities we share with all others, including those we teach and those we lead.

We need to be reminded that our physical beings must be nurtured and strengthened to support the soul, and only then can we fully support and teach others. This is no easy task, as the world of the teacher is one with increasing societal expectations and decreasing systems of support. But as difficult as that often is, it can lead to increased knowledge, wisdom, and tolerance—and a surprising amount of joy, if we position ourselves right.

First and foremost, a teacher is a spiritual being. Next, a teacher is a human being, and only if those are truly connected does the teacher become a true master. This is because a true master teacher is one who can connect with fellow humans in a pure and authentic way.

In this book, you will learn the specifics of the Seven Stages of Enlightenment for teachers, what Stage you are in, and how to advance to the next. It is an actual guide to spiritual development. Each Stage is presented with its own chapter and begins with a case study. Each individual presented as a case study is a composite of real people. The composites were put together to provide the most clear and vibrant portrayal of the facets of each Stage, and you will clearly recognize yourself and others.

Following the case study for each Stage is a reflection section that helps you explore whether that is the Stage you are in and want to be in. The gifts and challenges are explored for each of the Stages in such areas as worldview, relationships, and approach to teaching. This section also specifically addresses how the teacher at this Stage uses what Robert Marzano (2003) refers to us the "three teacher-level factors" (p. 76) of student achievement: instructional strategies, classroom management, and classroom curriculum design.

Finally, the presentation of each Stage ends with instructions on how to move on to the next Stage of Enlightenment through the use of specific professional skills and dispositions, as well as guided spiritual activities and rituals, including specific prayers, meditations, and journaling.

Meditation is a time for you to stop obsessing over what you need and want and actually take the time to listen. It is the paying of attention to that which arises from your own mind, your soul, that still small voice, the collective unconscious, spiritual guides, angels, or God. This is the time to connect with your own religious beliefs in a way that leaves you receptive to a higher power. Your job simply is to hear and to be aware. To have your heart and mind be open to what can awaken inside of you and what you can hear and learn. Consider the words of Ralph Waldo Emerson in Self Reliance:

> For the sense of being which in calm hours arises, we know not how, in the souls, is not diverse from things, from space, from light, from time, from man, but one with them and proceeds obviously from the same source whence their life and being also proceed. We first share the life by which things exist and afterwards see them as appearance in nature and forget that we have shared their cause. We lie in the lap of immense intelligence, which makes us receivers of its truth and organs of its activity.

You also are encouraged to incorporate music into your daily life, and specific styles of music are recommended for each of the various spiritual Stages. The music suggested is not meant to replace that to which you listen already, and it is not all inclusive to what is helpful at that Stage. It is to give you an idea of what type of music taps into that Stage's essential energy.

Feel free to explore, but take a moment to listen to a suggested piece, or something very similar. Sometimes a style is recommended—such as an adagio—sometimes an artist, sometimes a specific piece. Have fun with this exploration and follow your intuition. Music has a unique ability to draw us into ourselves. Plato said that "music is the movement of sound to reach the soul for the education of its virtue" and Victor Hugo said that "music expresses that which cannot be said and on which it is impossible to be silent."

Equipped with an understanding of these Stages, divine guidance, and a commitment to support your own soul and its path, you can methodically improve all aspects of your teaching life. As you make these changes, you will find that you will become happier, energized, more successful with your students, and more complete and confident as a person. Your life will improve!

There are teachers who have made it to the fifth, sixth and seventh Stages, and many more will join them. I hope this book helps. The engagement, inspiration, confidence, and wisdom imparted to the students of such teachers are the stuff that changes lives and the world. But, equally important is what happens to the teacher, for these Stages demonstrate two things: there is no division between teaching and the rest of life, and there is no division between us and God.

SPIRITUALITY, GOD, AND THE SOUL

Before embarking on a discussion of the Seven Stages, it is necessary for us to look at the whole concept of spirituality.

While spirituality is more or less an everyday word now, we need to establish a common understanding of its usage to best discuss the Stages of enlightenment through which teachers advance.

Spirituality is first and foremost the recognition that there is something beyond what we see and comprehend, and the belief there is something greater—more powerful, more loving—than us and the roles we play on earth.

Spirituality begins internally and prompts us to ask the questions that religions arise to answer. Author and religious scholar Thomas Moore (1993), who is more familiar with spiritual development than most, defines spirituality as "an aspect of any attempt to approach or attend to the invisible factors in life and to transcend the personal, concrete, finite particulars of this world" (p. 232).

Teacher and author James Moffett (1994) offers a definition that is more personalized by telling us that to be spiritual "is to perceive our oneness with everybody and everything and to act on this perception. It is to be whole within oneself and with the world" (p. xix).

When we think about Moffett's definition, we see that spirituality is simultaneously a condition and a process. It is a description of what we are as well as what we aim to be. This is where the understanding of the Seven Stages comes in. These Stages track and guide a teacher along an individual path from oneness to oneness-with-others, from seeing one's place in the world to seeing oneness-with-the-world.

A discussion of spirituality naturally leads to a discussion of God and the soul. Spirituality, as we have seen, is either a path or a goal, or both. And, this prompts us to ask if there is some aspect of ourselves that leads us, accompanies us, or is the "true" us as we embark down this path toward this goal.

There is widespread agreement that there is a something else to us, a something that walks and talks with God, something beyond the body. Kahlil Gibran (1993) said of his soul "My soul is my counsel and has taught me to give ear to the voices which are created neither by tongues nor uttered by throats."

However, the precise meaning of soul differs around the world and across religions, and it therefore deserves some attention here. For our purposes, it matters little what definition of soul you adhere to, but I suspect that you will need a belief in some definition of a soul in order to make sense of, and progress though, the seven stages presented in this book.

Jung believed that we do not strive for wholeness, rather we are born whole and spend our lives developing this wholeness to the greatest degree of harmony and coherence possible. This wholeness must, I believe, invariably include our souls. The ultimate goal of our soul, therefore, is to communicate with God in order to determine how best to combine our heart's desire and our purpose on earth.

The major religious traditions hold various, albeit similar, views of the soul and particularly the goal or path of the soul. Within each of these traditions are branches that further define the soul, particularly the mystical branches that seek and experience direct communication between soul and God.

For traditional Christians, the soul is generally seen as separate from the body with an existence that continues after the body has died. When the body dies, the soul either goes to heaven or to hell. In Islam the soul also is believed to exist separate from the body, and it seeks enlightenment. Hindus believe in a soul that is separate from the body and is one with that which is beyond definition. They see the ultimate goal of the soul as not wanting an attachment to a body. Judaism describes the soul as the nonphysical essence of a being. Buddhists see the soul as made up of dynamic energy seeking to reawaken the self. Its existence is not separate from the human form.

The soul therefore has a key role in our enlightenment as it brings us closer to God or to an understanding of God. What then is God? The concept of God is personally experienced, so I have taken great care to use a concept of God that is easily understood, if not universally accepted.

The idea that there could be a universal concept of God is supported by the fact that prominent religious traditions themselves have a multitude of descriptors for God, and yet, speak of one entity. St. Thomas Aquinas (1225–1274 CE) points out several names for God, all taken from scripture. The Hindu *Baghavad Gita* says that God has a million faces, and a Muslim tradition asks the practitioner to recite the ninety-nine most beautiful names for God (Fox, 2000).

A universal concept of God does not mean God is definable. In fact, I would say that God is undefinable. Any attributes we would give God immediately limit him, and thereby makes him "not God" because these are human concepts bounded by *our* thoughts and language. Further, God cannot be known objectively. As Kierkegarrd (1813–1855 CE) put it, the things we can grasp objectively are not the things that really matter to us, so if we can objectively grasp God, then it is not really God, therefore we have to grasp God through our faith.

For the purpose of this book, God is best understood as that which nothing greater can be conceived and which subsumes everything in existence, including space and time. God therefore is inseparable from us and as a result is omniscient and omnipresent. God has no beginning and no end. He is the "unmoved mover" (Aristotle, 384–322 BCE) and the original purpose behind the purpose of all things (Spinoza, 1632–1677 CE). Despite the need to use a gender pronoun in the English language, God has no gender.

God is knowable through his creations, the laws of nature, and mystical experiences. Einstein claimed to see God "in the wonderful order and lawfulness of all that exists and in its soul as it reveals itself in man and animal" (letter to Eduard Busching as cited in Jammer, 1999, p. 51), and all major religions and spiritual traditions have a mystical component that accepts an awareness of God through personal experience.

It is clear that a discussion of our souls, God, and our spiritual development will resonate with persons of various religious views. The variety of beliefs within and among the different religions does not limit an understanding of the spiritual stages within this book, but rather, is one of the reasons that the stages can be uniquely, and therefore authentically, navigated. The stages are not limited by, nor do they limit, religious beliefs and practices.

BECOMING A GREAT TEACHER

The teacher we each strive to be is one who inspires greatness within self and others. We can see this person in our mind's eye: personally confident, globally charitable, deeply content, and fully engaged with students.

This teacher is happy and at peace because she controls her own destiny. She connects with each and every one of her students, and she earns their respect and honor for the compassion and trust she demonstrates and evokes. She smiles with fondness at each of her fellow teachers and empathizes without judgment. She is present in her work. Her spirit walks with God, and her heart guides her students. But, she did not arrive at this place overnight. She grew as a person, teacher, and spiritual being. She moved upward through stages of greater awareness, understanding, commitment, and competence.

The Seven Stages are spiritual in their construct and can be identified, described, and analyzed under the following names: Searcher, Competitor, Protector, Mentor, Creator, Leader, and Healer. Every aspect of your life can be viewed and understood from the Seven Stages, from your views of self to your views of the world; from the management of your classroom to your choice in curriculum and lessons; from your relationships in your family to your relationships with your colleagues and your students.

These stages are evolutionary and accumulative. As you move from one stage to another, you shed those aspects of yourself that have been limiting your happiness, your effectiveness with students, and your spiritual growth. But, each stage is not merely a rung on a ladder; each has a fruitful side, and those fruits need to accompany you to your next stage.

As a matter of fact, you will not be able to fully advance into the next stage without recognizing and being grateful for the beauty you encountered and created while in the previous stage—as well as the challenges and difficult lessons. Faith and imagination are born of our past and must be honored if we are to create the future we desire.

You also will not be able to fully advance without believing you can. That is what Goethe understood when he said "Whatever you can do or imagine, begin it; boldness has beauty, magic, and power in it." The magic and power come directly from the first step.

While a teacher generally can be put into one stage, this is not always the case. While developing intellectually and spiritually, you may find that you move back and forth between stages. You may even find that you simultaneously are in a couple of different stages.

For instance, due to a new promotion, you may find yourself in a Mentor relationship with your peers and as a Searcher in relation to other administrators. During times of personal or professional stress, you may find yourself slipping back to a stage you previously mastered and then outgrew.

This is nothing to worry about. It is a safe and familiar place to be while sorting through confusing options or dealing with pain. If you see this happening to yourself, rely on what you learned about yourself from the previous stage and reacquaint yourself with the steps that moved you to the next. You quickly will move back onto the part of your path you were previously on—but with the added benefit of knowing more about yourself.

Think in terms of a musician. When a musician is struggling with a new composition, she will think nothing of taking some time to practice with old familiar pieces—even scales. And, when your students return after the long summer break, you ease them in by reviewing what they learned the previous spring, and you never judge them while doing so.

You do not move on to the next stage of development by eradicating the negative aspects of the current stage. Rather, you relieve yourself of the negative aspects of the current stage by moving forward to the next one. Reread those last two sentences.

The act of moving is what improves your situation and advances you forward. This may *sound* obvious, but if you look at your own life as well as those lives around you, you will see that this is not how people generally behave. We do more planning than acting, and we do more fixing than building. You need to keep your eye on the prize in order to move away from your flaws. This is the same thing a driving instructor will tell a student if she loses control of her car: "Don't look where you are going, look where you want to go, and that is where you will end up."

This does not mean you do not attend to your faults and those aspects of yourself that have created more challenges than blessings. As a matter-of-fact, you cannot steer yourself to the next stage unless you have come to appreciate what you are moving away from and why. Just as the driver's intent in a spin-out is to gain control of the car, your intent throughout the stages of spiritual development should be to gain control of your life by learning what the obstacles are in the particular stage, and then keeping your eyes and intentions elsewhere.

Always remember that you have the ability to understand your challenges, gain control of situations, make improvements to yourself, and truly be happy. This is a natural process for the spiritual beings we are.

THE SPIRITUAL CREST

Have you heard people talk about manifesting what they desire? How about discussions about quantum physics and how to use the universe to fulfill your dreams—have you heard those? In this section I will give you more details on the spiritual crest; how spiritual masters ride it; and how you can use the Seven Stages to quickly and gracefully change your life for the better.

Since the Seven Stages are spiritual in nature, advancing from one to another will include spiritual practices such as prayer, reflection, meditation, journaling, body movement, and music. These practices will vary from stage to stage, but all will rely on the understanding and use of a spiritual orientation that I have termed "The Crest."

The Crest is a state we enter when we consciously employ our body and soul to combine our talents, purpose, and personal desires for greater service to ourselves and others. It is a powerful place to be, but to get there takes nothing more than the alignment of these seven elements: mind, body, soul, talents, purpose, desires, and service. And the alignment takes nothing more than intent.

The Crest is a state of greater awareness. By focusing on the seven elements above you are rewarded with a more clear perspective and understanding of the issues in your life. This is amplified—and you are able to manifest your desires—when gratitude and forgiveness are fully engaged.

You know you are on The Crest when everything comes more peacefully and easily, you are content and understand your place in the world, and the answers to decisions unfold in front of you as if presented by an invisible hand. This is so much the case that people on The Crest often claim that choices and goals that seemed daunting and even impossible suddenly seemed like comfortable and logical next steps. There is an incredible sense of certainty and satisfaction on The Crest.

Being on The Crest is a lot like surfing an ocean crest. Just as when a surfer rides a wave, when you are on The Crest, you are moving quickly with a great view, but you have to pay close attention to your focus and balance. This means that you have to be responsive and agile and ready to move when the signs dictate that it is time to move. Sometimes these signs are physical, sometimes visual, sometimes intuitive, and sometimes divinely inspired. By listening to them, you know when to leave a job, take a job, engage or disengage in a relationship, or change lifestyle habits.

The Crest is all encompassing. When riding The Crest, you have a great view of what is in front of you and around you. You are riding on a higher plane, and that gives you the ability to "see" what is coming next, as well as possible future landscapes—depending upon what you steer toward.

Of course, you cannot see all possible options on your path, and that is why the balance and focus are so important. You need to triangulate the information you are receiving. Try to understand it from several different ways of knowing—what you see, what you feel, what you remember, what others have taught you, and what you hear through divine intervention.

Just like a surfer, you have to be continuously adjusting yourself and your orientation with the environment around you, and you have to realize your experience is incomplete and fleeting. You need to trust yourself in every second rather than think that the sea will never change. As Socrates taught us, the truly wise are those who know that they do not know.

The Crest is a place where intuition, insight, and coincidence are expected, but it is more than the "spiritual power," which M. Scott Peck defines as "capacity to make decisions with maximum awareness" (p. 285), because we move this capacity into deployment. We pay close attention to our bodies and what they tell us. We listen to the tension in our muscles, we listen to our cravings and desires, and we listen to the perceptions picked up by all of our senses and through each of our organs, not just our brains. We become an integrated whole. That is the balance necessary for staying on The Crest.

Getting on The Crest is easier in the final three stages of the Seven Stages, but all people can utilize this spiritual technique for advancement. The Crest is the primary reason some people move so quickly through the stages. Because each stage provides greater skills that increase intent, faith, and changes of habit, your balance and agility continue to improve.

Staying on The Crest is easier than it might seem. Keeping one's balance is always easier than gaining one's balance. It does necessitate spiritual discipline and mindfulness to stay integrated and on The Crest, but when you do so you will see that you are able to manifest your desires.

Believing is seeing. If you pay attention to the manifesting and do not assume that it is either dumb luck or some special blessing conferred upon you, you will find reward enough to stay put. Joseph Campbell describes the situation this way: " . . . if you follow your bliss you put yourself on a kind of track that has been there all the while, waiting for you, and the life that you ought to be living is the one you are living. When you see that, you begin to meet people who are in the field of your bliss, and they open the doors to you" (p. 150).

Stage 1

The Searcher

The spirit seeks to be broken through by God. God leads this spirit into a desert into the wilderness and solitude of the divinity where God is pure unity and where God gushes up within himself.

—Meister Eckhart

NAOMI

Naomi is a tiny woman with piercing dark eyes that seem to study everything. Her small stature combined with her long curly hair makes her almost indistinguishable from her students, and I get the feeling that her quick, darting movements are a way for her to bring attention to herself and thereby gain control of the classroom.

When she does gain control of her class, it is with an authoritative demand for attention. The class slowly, very slowly, comes around to give her their attention. And, while there is some restlessness and eye rolling, one gets the sense that the students respect Naomi and are ready to learn from her.

Naomi has been teaching for nine years now, but often she refers to herself as a new teacher. "I know nine years is a long time, I mean, I am only thirty-two years old . . . I've been teaching my whole adult life. But, I feel like a rookie, even a poser. I feel like every other teacher in the world knows something I don't know."

We all feel like this at some time—as if we are faking it while the rest of the world is mastering "it." For Naomi, there is a bit more reality to the situation. This is because she has moved around in her teaching career so much that she has not developed a common understanding with a group of people,

11

which is necessary in order to establish a sense of community, and eventually a sense of mastery within a community.

Her first job out of college was as a teacher in a suburban elementary school. She was jazzed when she first started, with stars in her eyes as bright as those in the third-graders she taught. "The job was easy," Naomi explains, "I was as happy teaching as they were learning." She pauses. "But, it wasn't enough. I worked hard, but soon I didn't really feel challenged." After one year, Naomi left.

Naomi was looking for more, but she was not looking for more work or harder days. She was searching for more challenge. What did that mean?

For Naomi it meant that she wanted to make a difference on a larger stage. She did not just want to help these particular third-graders learn their multiplication tables; she wanted to help humankind. She did not just want the lives of these students to be improved; she wanted the world to be improved. And, more importantly, she wanted feedback that this was happening.

She did not just want to rely on faith. She wanted to see more than the ripple her pebble caused. She wanted to see all of the ripples and how they merged. Naomi had all of the care and optimism we want in our teachers, but she was not getting the feedback for which she hungered. After her first job with suburban third-graders, Naomi worked at an inner-city charter school. She was confident that working with inner-city kids would bring the fulfillment she was looking for. After all, she surmised, there could not be a place where she would be more challenged, or more needed and appreciated.

It was true that she was needed, and she was appreciated by many students and teachers. Unfortunately, Naomi did not know it. That is because she never believed that she fit in with the other teachers at the school. They were primarily teachers of color, Hispanic and Black, and many of them had grown up in the neighborhood, or a replica in another big city. "I am not one of them," she would tell her friends. "They are so patronizing to me. They don't think I know anything about these kids."

Her friends convinced her that she was not appreciated and that her fellow teachers did not believe she "got it," because they were "closed minded." Naomi did not know what these teachers thought of her because she never asked, and she never got to know them beyond their roles.

To no one's surprise, the unhappy, but deeply loyal Naomi stayed at the inner-city charter school for three years—complaining to her family and friends the entire time, but providing steady direction and discipline to her students. She learned a lot about teaching and her appreciation for diversity deepened. She grew a lot in her three years at this school, but she was personally disconnected most of the time and looked back at those years as lost years.

When she started looking for a different place to teach, Naomi sought something safe and familiar. She decided to check out her place of worship—a place where she knew everyone and everyone knew her—a place where she already fit in. She was enthusiastically hired as a high school teacher at the school run by her synagogue.

Naomi enjoyed her new position. She was especially comfortable with the hierarchy and the rules the Jewish establishment infused into the high school. She knew what was expected of her and her students. She knew where to go if she had a concern or a complaint. Most of the students were well-behaved with active parents.

Naomi had found a place where she really could concentrate on being the best teacher possible. She was not sure how she was influencing the larger world, but she knew that Judaism was about making a difference in lives so she had faith in her role within this larger community. "I know these kids will soon be using what I have taught them. I can see that I am making a difference with them and feel as if I can see how they are going to make a difference in the world. Some of these kids are just amazing."

Naomi was specifically excited about her (Distributive Education Clubs of America) DECA kids. Determined to make a contribution to this high school, Naomi started a DECA chapter for the students, and it was very successful. It was successful in part because Naomi was able to talk with many of the students and their parents at synagogue. She also was able to match-up many of the DECA kids with business people from the synagogue and neighboring community. It all came together, her faith, her career, and her community. Her world made sense, and that is very important to a Searcher-teacher. She even started dating a man from her synagogue.

David was a kind and quiet man, an easy stereotype for the accountant he was. He also made sense: he was predictable and dependable—a reflection of what a Searcher desires. During her third year of teaching at the Jewish school, Naomi felt the familiar unrest. "It snuck up the way it usually did. One minute I was happy, the next minute I was not . . . am not."

Naomi thought she was bored. The rules and unbending system she was so fond of initially, now seemed archaic. When she met with secular teachers at professional development events, they often were critical of her school and the lack of educational choices the students were given in order to complete their Jewish studies. When Naomi would defend the school as "no different than Catholic schools," the response was one version or another of "exactly."

Naomi did not think she had found success where she thought success was assured, and she certainly was not receiving the validation from her friends that she so desperately sought. She was demoralized and ashamed of herself, primarily because she was quick to adopt the perspective of her "tribe"—the friends with whom she chose to associate, and to whom she gave personal power in exchange for a needed sense of community and security.

Naomi had become a more experienced teacher, and she wanted respect from her teaching peers. She also wanted to prove to herself that she could fit in and be happy. She finished her third year at the Jewish high school, and took a job at an urban high school. This was a high school filled with promise and need: it was a high school where more than eighty languages and dialects were spoken by the students; it was a place where the poverty rate and special education rate mirrored third-world countries.

This was a place where it was easy to get a job and easy to hide. This is where we find Naomi now. She is in her second year teaching English, and she knows that she left her last two jobs after her third year. "My friends . . . David . . . everyone expects me to be somewhere else after next year. Maybe they are right. Maybe I should be looking for another job. I am not happy here. There is not enough money for the classroom. Some of the teachers don't even like to teach, and God knows many of the parents don't want to parent. The principal is in way over her head, and the school board is some committee in the sky as far as I am concerned."

Naomi explains that she is ready to move on to another school, and her arms are folded and posture defensive when she states that "there is nothing wrong with looking for the perfect job."

She is quiet for a couple of minutes, and then looks out into the distance as she softly utters "one day my sister said to me 'whereever you go, there you are.' I hated her for saying it to me, but I understood it to my core. Maybe I am someone who just can't be satisfied."

That is the danger in being a Searcher-teacher. You are seeking *self*-satisfaction outside your*self*. Maybe she is right. But this can change for Naomi, and for you if you are anything like her. Naomi can learn to live with herself, but first she needs to believe that this does not have to include living with discontent and unhappiness. Naomi is a Searcher, and she has two choices. She can continue to be a Searcher and learn to find peace at this stage by understanding that the judgment of others and unrest will be constant companions, or she can move on to the next stage and begin down a path of personal fulfillment and joy.

ARE YOU A SEARCHER-TEACHER?

Can you relate to Naomi's circumstances? Do you empathize with her struggles? Do you find yourself searching for something more—something that feels like validation—an assurance that you are okay?

If you are a young teacher, you are probably a Searcher. Most Searchers in the field of education are our young teachers. That is no surprise because there is a maturational component to the spiritual stages. In other words, it is pretty difficult to find yourself at Stage Five never having been at Stage Four.

Young people in particular have a searching aspect to themselves as they try to figure out what they want to do for a living, where they want to live, and whom they want as a life partner. If you also are new to teaching, you are of course discovering what teaching style suits you best, what ages you most easily reach, and what curriculum type you are most comfortable applying. Each of these ventures is entwined with the development of self, and as we will learn in this book, the act of teaching is a spiritual act making the educational discoveries of a teacher, personal spiritual discoveries.

Anyone at any age can find herself in the Searcher Stage, and indeed, many people remain there. If you are a seasoned teacher who reads this chapter and believes herself to be at the Searcher Stage, you should not view this as negative. It merely means you have over-developed an aspect of yourself and neglected others. You have much more to discover about your own gifts and abilities.

As you move forward through the Stages, you will find solutions to problems you did not even know you had, in the same way you sometimes do not know you are hungry until you smell the food. You also should realize that it is not easy to move out of the Searcher Stage—or any Stage for that matter—without self-reflection and determination to do so. Our society tends to focus on goals rather than on the journey, so the Searchers among us are particularly disadvantaged as they do not receive much support. Ironically, this causes many of them to remain in this Stage. They do not receive support for being Searchers and little support for the search. Rather, they tend to receive pity and prodding, which tends to immobilize them. Since they appear never to be satisfied, their friends and relatives grow weary of their constant discontent, and support for their endeavors further dwindles.

The lack of support from friends and relatives is especially difficult for a Searcher because her continuous searching has likely left her isolated from society at large and more dependent on her small circle of friends and relatives.

You might also find yourself in the Searcher Stage after a life crisis. This is a comfortable stage for regrouping, reprioritizing, or refuge seeking. If you find yourself in this Stage after just such an event, be gentle with yourself and know that you will be able to bounce back rather quickly to your immediately previous Stage—as soon as you want to. In a situation such as this, it is unlikely that you will need to go through stages that you already have gone through prior to your crisis. But allow yourself to take the path of least resistance. When we go back to a stage and retrace our steps forward, we can learn new things that improve our spiritual development and our general outlook on life.

Searcher-teachers are very earthbound, and much of their energy will go into concern for their own basic needs as well as those of their immediate family. This concern is based in a survival instinct that causes the Searcher-teacher to worry about the future as much as the present. This divides a Searcher's energy further than her capacity, not only between her home and her classroom, but also between the here and now and the infinite possibilities for both.

Although you may find, as a Searcher-teacher, that you are caught up in daily needs and often are self-absorbed, it does not mean you do not have the capacity to care for others. In fact, you have a great deal of respect for those close to you, and this most notably is seen in your treatment of them especially the nurturing of your own students. However, you do tend to see through group eyes and can therefore become intolerant of those whose views are different from yours, or who suddenly grow out of favor when they venture out of your comfort zone.

A Searcher-teacher's circle of friends will be small, intimate, and like minded, and cultivating this group takes some time. The Searcher will constantly be looking for the right group in which to belong in every environment, and she will most assuredly use other people she already knows to make the introductions. To her benefit, her natural curiosity about herself, her surroundings, and her friends will provide a good foundation for learning and growth.

To determine whether you are a Searcher-teacher, the first and most helpful place to look is at your view of yourself. Are you often disappointed with yourself? Are you discontented with your life in general? Are you preoccupied with day-to-day survival—namely your finances and your health?

As we saw with Naomi, when people are in the Searcher Stage they are frustrated with themselves. Most of us know when we are frustrated with ourselves, but we do not always take the time to stop and assess further. While the frustration eventually will go away, it might not be because the problems went away. It could be that we just habituated them, lessening our own frustration in the process.

For spiritual growth, this is not sufficient. You need to understand the source of your frustration and ameliorate it, if not eradicate it. As difficult as it is, you must set aside the quiet time that is necessary for both self understanding and spiritual growth. This is the case regardless of which Stage you are in, but it becomes second nature as you advance through the Stages. So, for optimal spiritual growth, reflection needs to become part of your lifestyle as early in the spiritual growth process as possible.

As you seek to determine your view of yourself, listen to the words you use to describe yourself and your situation. Looking at the language we use to define and describe ourselves is very telling. A Searcher primarily is concerned with two predominant things: what others think of her and determining what she should care about.

If you are a Searcher-teacher you might find that you continuously seek the approval of others. You want to be validated for what you have done and who you are. You also seek to discover what it is that should matter to you. Unfortunately, you all too readily seek this information through others. You might find yourself asking of others such questions as "why do you care about that?" "why do you care what she thinks?" "why do you believe that?" and "how do you know that?"

It is true that you will want to move beyond needing the approval and validation of others, but the positive aspect of needing to understand the feelings and beliefs of others is that you eventually will use this information to try to improve yourself—that is, if you seek to improve yourself.

If you find that you are prompted to ask these questions because you really are wondering about what others care about, you are doing so in part so that you can determine what you may be missing in yourself. This curiosity is a gift to the Searcher as well as to those she queries because it causes both parties to give more appreciation to the things they care about and more analysis to what they do not seem to care about.

Changing jobs frequently is a solid indication that you are a Searcher. A Searcher is looking for a place to belong, and naturally where one spends forty to sixty hours per week is a critical place to start. To determine whether your job searching is an indication of being a Searcher you should first analyze what drives you to look for a new position. Do not look solely at what you tell others, because we all fall into the trap from time to time of presenting ourselves in a manner that aligns with the expectations of the person to whom we are speaking, even if that alignment skews reality a bit.

If you change positions every couple of years because you are seeking more responsibility or trying to get to a particular geographical location this is not an indication that you are a Searcher. Searchers do not change paths toward a particular destination, they are changing paths as they change destinations, and they change destinations to feel appreciated and to gain a sense of belonging.

Do you change positions because you "just don't fit in," because you "are not appreciated," or because you would rather stay home sick than go to work, but you really cannot put your finger on why? Those feelings would indicate that you are a Searcher.

Your Strengths

Even though it is the first spiritual stage of teacher development, there are many positive aspects to the Searcher-teacher.

Seeking is a fun and noble act. Enjoying the act of seeking, in and of itself, is something you do not want to lose as you move through the Stages. A Searcher-teacher is asking the questions that really matter: who am I and what do I want? And while she is not yet relying sufficiently on herself and a higher power for the answers, the earnestness with which she asks is one that you will want to carry with you throughout your spiritual development.

If you are a true Searcher you know that you can be deeper and more complex than someone who just wants more of the same; you can be someone who seeks the essence in everything you do. By essence, I mean that part of a person, object, or event that makes it unique and that offers something in particular to the person who encounters it. It is the same thing that separates a tourist from a traveler. You can see a site, or you can understand a site. You can appreciate its beauty, or you can appreciate its beauty in light of its historical relevance and cultural significance.

Searcher-teachers usually have a sense of newness and freshness that the rest of us would benefit from remembering and employing. Because change is a regular part of their lives, they pop into environments and situations with a new and generally objective perspective. Searcher-teachers may not have a clear view of themselves, but they can have a clear view of their surroundings.

If you are a Searcher-teacher, have confidence in what you observe and what you believe you understand about a situation. Be ready to share your views, but do so from a perspective that is removed from "what can this do for me?" There will be time for that too, but take the opportunity to improve what is around you first.

Your Challenges

Because the Searcher-teacher is caught up in a cycle of searching and not finding, she has not adequately developed trust, especially in herself. This becomes a vicious cycle. As a Searcher-teacher, you see yourself on a path, not at a destination, and so this is what you continuously put in front of yourself—a path, which is more steps, more obstacles, more sites along the way. It is important to enjoy life's journey, but in order to grow physically, mentally, emotionally, and spiritually, you must arrive at particular destinations along the way.

This starts with defining where you want to be, determining the shortest way to get there—not the longest, and then trusting that you will arrive. This may seem like common sense, but it is the nature of a Searcher-teacher to find the longest path, and it is the nature of most of us to lack the faith that we will ever arrive at our heart's desires. We settle for substitutes and replicas because we think we have to. We let our history, or more specifically, the history of our parents, define our goals. As a Searcher-teacher you have a tendency to not adequately take responsibility for your decisions. As such, you often will see yourself as a victim of circumstances or of decisions made by others—decisions you let them make or assumed they made.

Your Relationships

The Searcher-teacher is driven by her need to fit in and belong. She can be open-minded, yet easily influenced by others. Her concern with belonging brings about deep loyalty to close friends and family, but it also can create dependency upon them and their beliefs. As a Searcher-teacher, you may find that, even the gentlest of your judgments of others is based on how they compare to what your family has set forth as right, proper, and ethical. If your key relationships are with other Searchers, those can develop into codependent alliances. You need to be watchful.

To a Searcher-teacher, family plays the most important role in her decision-making. If you are a Searcher-teacher, regardless of your age, you probably feel compelled to run past your parents all major decisions in your life, and in a marital relationship, there is a danger that your spouse will either be ignored, or will take on a surrogate parental role.

You are quick to subordinate your interest in order to give others control over you for things over which you would prefer not to have power. This is where the codependency starts developing and how you begin abdicating control of your own life. It seems comfortable to give someone else power over your decisions, but ultimately, it stunts your spiritual growth as well as the growth of your relationships.

As a Searcher-teacher, you view yourself as an honorable person who has not yet found her place and who is not yet appreciated. You have some idea of what you do not know, and you want to use education as a means to improve yourself as well as provide a career.

All of us seek happiness, and while a Searcher-teacher often will believe that the world is against her, or the time is not right for her, or she is in the wrong place at the wrong time, she does believe, as Aristotle (384–322 BCE) did, that one must use all of her abilities and capabilities to achieve happiness. As a Searcher-teacher, you might enjoy the teachings of Aristotle, especially his Nicomachean Ethics. But, also consider the parable Jesus told of the ten talents (Mt 25:14–30). You have a strong work ethic, even though you job-hop, so it is helpful to focus on situations that get you thinking of how best to utilize your gifts and how to accept and achieve abundance.

The Searcher-teacher will gravitate to persons with strong personalities. She might admire their courage, she might seek to learn from their confidence, or she might long to be cajoled or coerced down a particular path. The Searcher-teacher can be exploited if she does not recognize that this orientation creates vulnerability. As pointed out earlier, the Searcher-teacher is too quick to give her limited personal power over to others whom she believes to be more skilled, capable, or connected.

Similarly, if the Searcher-teacher is not careful, she can objectify and use other people. This is because, as someone who is preoccupied with daily needs and basic happiness, she is self-absorbed. She does not easily empathize with the plight of others, looking instead through her own limited-view lenses. This is another reason to accept a more abundant view of the world. Do not think of the things you want as scarce. Work to believe that there is enough of everything for everyone. You might be able to cite facts that disprove this, but this is a spiritual book, and it is about belief systems and how they influence reality, and vice versa.

Your World

If you are a Searcher-teacher, your view of self manifests itself clearly in the kind of environment you prefer. It is important to Searchers to fit in, but they are rigid and dogmatic in much of their thinking, so they do not easily fit in with groups they have not personally assembled or been introduced into. This causes them to believe that they function best when they are isolated. In a sense, this is true. In isolation, they can concentrate on the task at hand rather than worrying about how they are being viewed and accepted by their peers.

While this may seem to be ideal, it generally is problematic. An isolated Searcher is flying without a compass. She may be happy and productive in her classroom with the door tightly shut, but she is not developing. The Searcher-teacher has not turned inward and has not learned to rely on her own abilities. Therefore, she actually needs the reflection provided by others. Unfortunately an isolated classroom takes her away from this necessary influence and guidance of other teachers.

If you seek isolation because you do not want to worry about what others think of you, then you probably are a Searcher-teacher. Eventually, in other Stages of development you may seek isolation, but it will not be because you are worried about what others think of you. As a Searcher-teacher, try to avoid isolation.

Your worldview focuses a lot on what is right and wrong, from politics to religion, and it is based on its congruence to how you were raised and of what your parents and religious elders would approve. Each of these systems is rigid and well-organized in your mind's ideal with roles to be played and rules to be obeyed by all. If you are loving and loyal to your family and have confidence in receiving the same from them, this rigidity in behavior will not seem restrictive to you, but rather consistent and supportive. If your family is well-functioning, that is without chemical abuse, mental illness, or abusive behaviors, this struc-ture can provide a solid foundation from which to develop.

However, if you do not work to intentionally move forward, you could find yourself in a life that disappears by decades without advancing your thinking and connection to God. There also is a danger that, without moving forward through the spiritual Stages, your limited worldview could become filtered through intolerance—anything from classism to nationalism.

Searcher-teachers often rely on their religions as the constant in their lives. They may change places of worship, but they are not likely to change religions or much of their beliefs. Also, Searchers enjoy the dependability of views and consistency of behaviors that come from traditional religions. A Searcher-teacher is someone comfortable with both dogma and doctrine and often will use these tools of religious traditions to build her worldview and instructional strategies.

As a Searcher-teacher, you prefer to be with people who share your beliefs and values. You believe that there are absolute truths that are, or can be, known by everyone. As a Searcher-teacher, your religious views are likely those passed down by your parents. A Searcher-teacher respects tradition and authority, and would not immediately question the views of those she respects—especially if those views are working successfully in their lives. You will accept and support a bureaucratic hierarchy, and while it is not likely that you will seek a position of power within this structure, you may seek out peripheral participation in auxiliary social groups.

Your Approach to Teaching

As an educator you can assess your spiritual Stage of development by look-ing closely at your personal view of education, which would include what you see as the purpose of education, how you interact with students, your relationships with your colleagues, the atmosphere in your classroom, and the curriculum you choose to use.

As a Searcher-teacher, your own reasons for becoming a teacher were more personal and immediate. But, if you were to take the time now to consider what you believe to be the purpose of education, you probably would be comfortable with one of the main theories you learned in college—that education is designed to transmit culture. For you, the Searcher, this would mean specifically the transmission of rules, ethics, and the basic skills a person would need in order to participate as a citizen without being a burden to society.

The instructional strategies used by a teacher are directly related to the Stage in which she finds herself. The Searcher-teacher is comfortable with order and predictability, and that can be seen in her instructional choices. So, you are most likely pragmatic, rule-oriented, and concerned with the basic skill development of your students. You probably prefer to use direct instruction where you have more control over what knowledge is imparted. You are confident in your own views and beliefs, and as such approach instruction in a didactic fashion.

Regardless of how much you like to control and regulate your classroom, you do enjoy developing a sense of community, so you likely try to incorporate structured meetings times such as homeroom, circle time, or the like.

The Searcher-teacher enjoys exploring the basics and the foundation of things. Therefore you will seek to find causal relationships and often teach your students using cause and effect examples. You also will rely on comparisons to make points, and you might utilize rote learning in order to assure memorization. Many of the techniques that you were exposed to in your own education will be most comfortable to you—including worksheets, drills, and paper and pencil tests. As instructional strategies have largely moved beyond these methods, you might still be trying to find a place for them.

You understand how critical it is for your students to be equipped with specific tools, and so you tend to emphasize skills and skill development. You believe that it is as important to acquire skills and knowledge in a timely manner as it is to acquire them. You therefore are apt to impose tests and strict time limits on them.

Searcher-teachers prefer classrooms that are orderly and limiting. Not only does this fit well with this developmental stage, it supports the instructional strategies that come naturally to Searchers. Many students, especially young ones and those from more toxic environments, will find security and comfort in the order and structure provided in this type of classroom. As a matter of fact, teacher and author Marva Collins (1992), whose teaching life was made into a movie, lists in her book behaviors students need from their teachers. Many of these come naturally to the Searcher, especially setting standards, providing discipline, offering help, being honest, and giving praise.

Still, there is much danger that as a Searcher-teacher you overly restrict your students' creativity and developing sense of self. Keep this in mind as you seek to improve your teaching as well as your spiritual development.

As a Searcher-teacher you keep a distance from your students. It is not that you do not touch them, especially the young ones who expect hugs and pats on the back, but you keep your emotional distance. You see your relationship as one-sided: you are there to provide to them, and they really have nothing to provide to you. This is a view that will change as you develop through the Stages. However, you take very seriously the nurturing and instruction you provide.

You have a deep respect for hierarchy even in your classroom, and you tend to use power to assure signs of respect. This is how, in your mind, you reach out to and support your students. Your classroom will be rule-oriented, and you may even have the rules posted in the classroom. Rules are a normal part of our society, and so there is nothing inherently negative about a list of rules, as long as the rules are fair, understandable, equally enforced, and revisited with student needs at the forefront—perhaps even with student input. As you move through the spiritual Stages, you will find yourself relying less on rules and more on respect.

It was pointed out earlier that as a Searcher-teacher you will gravitate toward curriculum that stresses the basic skills through drill and memorization. This is a result of key aspects of you and your comfort zone. For you, the goal, whether conscious or unconscious, is to transmit culture and this leads to a tendency to see everyone as more or less the same, and therefore you do not fully appreciate different learning styles. You will teach to the group and do so in a manner that is easily assessed by you—even if it is not the most accurate assessment of true student learning or a valid measure of student struggles.

You will have a tendency to adhere to strict timelines, even if this excludes some of your students. Your students will learn necessary discipline skills and the importance of deadlines and punctuality, but if you are dealing with either young children or children with challenges or risk factors, this approach could end up limiting what they are able to learn and produce for you. You need to carefully balance the comfort received from order and the challenges associated with rigidity—especially of timelines. You also need to keep in mind that the other Stages of spiritual development offer more democratic, egalitarian, and authentic forms of curriculum.

As a Searcher-teacher you would prefer curriculum that others create. You would see no need to reinvent the wheel or to challenge the work of experts. Given the need or requirement to develop your own curriculum, or build upon that which is given to you, your approach likely would be to rely directly on your own experience—what you were taught or what a mentor guided you through.

When it comes to assessing your students, you will prefer to focus on the basics and foundations. If you are a teacher in a classroom, you will see great merit in using multiple choice tests. Not only will you be able to clearly and cleanly determine who knows what, you will have the ability to crunch the numbers and determine readily what curricular topics might need further exploration in your class.

When it comes to subjects and topics, you are likely to find yourself focusing on such things as earth sciences and historical facts. You will be quite comfortable with courses where you can address and assess facts rather than analysis and opinions. When you allow yourself to be free with text and resource choices you will tend to focus on topics related to nationalism and patriotism. As a Searcher, you are particularly drawn to such tribal issues. You believe that a strong and homogeneous cultural, religious, and patriotic foundation is a key to a strong country. You are happy to impart such things to your students.

Moving from Searcher to Competitor

Life as a Searcher-teacher is both predictable and frenetic as the Searcher jumps from one structured environment to the next and from one reliable position or relationship to the next. The predictability will eventually become stifling if you seek to grow spiritually, and the frenetic pace will seem less like an adventure and more like you are a hamster in a wheel.

You will grow weary of being a Searcher-teacher, but fear of the unknown will keep you in this stage. Searchers do not like change and cause their own discontent as they continue to run away searching for undefined fulfillment. To move to the next stage of spiritual development requires you to embrace the unknown. Remind yourself that, although you don't like change, you often find yourself in it, so there is no reason to be fearful. And while it takes effort to move to the next stage, this book gives you the knowledge and the courage to do so.

Others keep you at the Searcher stage when they encourage your discontent, discourage your growth, or urge you to change that which is external, but not what is internal.

Most people would want to help a Searcher advance to the next stage because, if for no other reason, they have grown tired of hearing the same old Searcher lament of not feeling understood, appreciated, and utilized. However, the Searcher tends to associate with like-minded people in similar occupations making it more difficult to find fresh ideas and new solutions. When the Searcher is confronted with a new approach that could get her out of her rut and on to personal growth, she often recoils at the criticism seeing it as an indication that she has somehow failed to fit in, to be accepted.

It is time to move on to the next stage if you are seeking your authentic self rather than a place to belong, and if you are ready to give up the obstacles and embrace the gifts of the Searcher-teacher. This new search will take you inward and focus your attention on the calling of your higher consciousness and the spirit.

Maria Montessori said that "If Helen Keller attained through exquisite natural gifts to an elevated conception of the world, who better than she proves that in the inmost self of man lies the spirit ready to reveal itself?" (Montessori, 1965, p. 26). These are words for you to concentrate upon as you seek to move to the next stage.

The main obstacle that stands in the way of your advancement to the next stage is intolerance. You have not yet realized that all in the world are one. You tend to focus your attention on the differences among people and miss the sameness. You then see the differences as something in the other that needs to change. This tendency to be intolerant is exacerbated by your inability to take advice from others.

When others do try to counsel a Searcher, she does not really hear them. She is trying to make things fit into what she already believes, so she does not listen well to others. She tends to hear what she needs to hear in order to keep her system static. She wants to belong, but instead of analyzing what she really wants in life and looking for a place where she really will fit in, she looks for a place where she thinks she should fit in based on the values and views of her family and friends. Then she adjusts her image, not her core.

Since she does not know the true desires of her heart and soul, the Searcher only appears to be fitting in. This is the pattern you are in as a Searcher. When you are unable to reconcile the image others have of you with your authentic self, you grow discontented and seek to ease this discomfort by changing your environment rather than trying to understand yourself.

The main gift you have as a Searcher is your wonderful pragmatism. When you do decide to move forward spiritually, you are well-equipped to best figure out how to conquer your misgivings and get past the obstacles.

You are alert and curious, and you will enjoy a new direction and new search. Some of the greatest growth you will ever experience is at the end of the Searcher stage. To support yourself, use the structures with which you have surrounded yourself. Also, learn to see beyond roles. Searchers are quick to stereotype and to categorize, including people. Note this in yourself, and seek to change it. Build on your natural inclination to be loyal, but seek to broaden to whom you are loyal. See it as a trait that you possess rather than an action others have earned.

Balance is another aspect of yourself to nurture. Go back once again to the teachings of Aristotle and his discussions of the Golden Mean. It is the kind of balance and mediation of needs that gives you comfort and will provide for you a foundation on which to build. Trust in nature and celebrate the bounty of the earth. Consider taking up gardening or cooking in order to visibly see for yourself how you are cared for by the earth.

Believe that all is as it should be, and develop your religious faith around that concept. Do not regret any time you have spent as a searcher. Keep your eye on continuous improvement and growth based on your time as a Searcher. Believe that you are deserving of all that you desire.

In order to move to the next stage, you need to embrace the unknown and be ready to move forward, but you also must find peace where you are. At any given moment, and any stage of development, you must be thankful for who you are and where you are, and you must see the blessings before you.

Spiritual development is accumulative. Remember that you can have great influence where you are, even while looking to change. Begin to increase your faith in the unseen and in a life cared for. The Searcher-teacher who is ready to move on to the next stage is concerned with what it means to "be" in a world where all is one. She is beginning to understand that we all belong together on this planet, and any view of the world that seeks to separate us is illusory. She will recognize as Dorothy Day did that "in the long run all man's problems are the same, his human needs are for sustenance and love" (Day, p. 286).

Spend less time trying to make sense of your place and how others view you. Instead, focus on creating the place you want.

Incorporating the Right Changes

As you begin to make movement toward becoming a Competitor-teacher, you will want to incorporate instructional strategies that will support this movement as well as prepare you for aspects of yourself that will emerge or grow stronger in that stage.

You might want to start by creating learning contracts between you and each student where you articulate general expectations as well as clear learning objectives and progress goals. This is an opportunity for you to let go of some of the control of your students while still offering them clear expectations and firm deadlines.

It also would be helpful for you to add reflection time for the students after your direct instruction. This will give them time to truly digest and synthesize what you have presented to them. If you then have them share their thoughts, you will come to find a deeper understanding of what they have learned and how they viewed the lesson. If you want to really push yourself out of your comfort zone, consider creating more inner stability within the students by giving them self-knowledge exercises.

As a Searcher-teacher, you probably currently look for collegial organizations that unconsciously fulfill your need for a tribe. And when you fulfill this need to belong, you will experience great satisfaction, and as a result you will find that you do grow in these circumstances. Therefore, it might serve you well to seek out professional development in a venue that is ongoing. As for content, once you have decided to move forward, you should seek out professional development opportunities that teach you how to use games as instructional tools as well as other methods geared specifically toward student engagement.

You should also explore methods that give real life relevance to learning. For instance, if you are teaching math or economics, you might want to consider a stock exchange game. If you are a karate teacher, explore the historical origins of the sport.

Incorporating Spiritual Practices

Below are Stage-specific practices designed to do two things: they will honor and celebrate the Stage you are at, and they will prepare you for the expectations of the next Stage. While it is your goal to develop into more advanced Stages, this will happen more quickly if you express understanding and gratitude for the Stage in which you currently are. Full appreciation for the wonderful person you already have become is necessary for spiritual growth.

Searcher-teacher Prayer:

Thank you for another day.
Help those who are in pain, who are suffering,
and who do not have their daily needs met.
Guide me this day and all days on my path
that I may always know that I am loved and cared for,
not only by my family but by you.
Bless me with my daily needs for sustenance and happiness,
and let me not forget that you always will be there
guiding me, caring for me, and protecting me.
My life has a purpose,
and as I seek to better understand what it is,
keep me, my loved ones, and my students safe and prosperous.
Keep us out of harm's way,
and help us see your presence in the natural beauty around us.

Searcher-teacher Meditation:

You will need to read through this entire meditation before you begin. If you are able, do this meditation outdoors. And, regardless of the environment, try to sit on the floor or as close to the ground as you are able. Spend a couple of minutes with your mind blank. See what thoughts come to you. To begin your Searcher-teacher meditation, close your eyes and picture a bright red light in your mind.

Think back to a specific time in your childhood. Picture an event that made you very happy. Immerse yourself in this vision. See what you are wearing, look around at your surroundings, and take note of who else is there.

Try to feel the happiness that you felt at that particular time. Why are you happy? Take time to really think about what is causing your happiness. Now, think about how this happiness is related to your family, particularly your parents. Did they do something to make you happy? Are you excited to share with them your happiness? Are you in this environment because of their decisions? Make sure to find a connection with this happiness and your parents. Even if your relationship with one or both is conflicted, parents still have a role in our happiness, either directly or indirectly. Find their piece of your happiness in this situation.

Now, think about today. What part of your happiness today can be attributed back to your parents? Take a few minutes to think about all of the ways your parents have contributed to your happiness. Is it a sense of humor that you have gotten from them? Is it the joy they still bring to you? Is it a view of the world that you have learned from them? After you have spent some time relating your childhood as well as your adult happiness to your parents, take a moment to silently thank them in your head. If one or both are deceased, present this thank you to their spirits. Sit in the blessing of happiness and thankfulness.

Searcher-teacher Journaling

In your journal, make a list of your heart's desires. Now, write a sentence for each of these desires by filling the blank with your desire: "I am deserving of _____ because God loves me and wants me to enjoy the abundance of his world. I trust in God to know my desires and guide me to their fulfillment."

Create a new sentence every time you create a new desire. Go back and read these entries often, and seek to really believe them.

In your journal, make a list of your teaching fears. What are you most worried about? Where do you think you might fail? Now write those same fears again, but next to them write "all problems have solutions. I will find the right solution." Next to that, write three possible solutions.

As you do this, keep in mind that it is true that all problems have solutions, and that a higher power is guiding you toward the development of your solutions. Make a commitment to employ your solutions.

Searcher-teacher Movements

Build your muscles and your stamina so that you feel strong and able to support yourself physically. The Searcher-teacher, more than anyone, will benefit from even the modest improvements to physical health and strength.

Exercise and dance are important for physical as well as spiritual development. Try to move your body often and vigorously. Good activities for the Searcher are running, bicycling, floor exercises, and spontaneous dancing to a strong beat.

Searcher-teacher Music

The Searcher-teacher should listen to as much drumming as possible— especially when meditating or doing movements. Some suggested music is the following:

David and Steve Gordon, especially Sacred Drum Vision
Mickey Hart's Planet Drum
Evelyn Glennie
The Explorer Series: West African Drum, Chant and Instrumental Music

The Searcher-teacher is summarized in the table below.

Table 1.1

View of self	Struggling
Motivation	To fit in
Strengths	Loyal; dependable
Weaknesses	Codependant; paranoid
View of others	As more successful; as helpers
View of God, spirituality	View of God is limited. Religious views are based on views held by parents and religious leaders. Finding others who believe the same is most important. There are absolute truths, and they are known by others.
View of education	Transmit culture
Instructional strategies	Direct instruction, didactic instruction, drill, comparisons, copying, questions and answers
Classroom management	Through hierarchy, rules, rewards, and sanctions
Use of curriculum	Get basic facts across
Necessary to move a stage	Realize authentic self is rooted in the commonality of all people

Stage 2

The Competitor

I, God, am in your midst. Whoever knows me can never fall, Not in the heights, Not in the depths, Nor in the breadths, For I am love, Which the vast expanses of evil Can never still.

—Hildegard of Bingen

CAROLL

When asked how he likes being a big fish in a small pond, Caroll responds "I would be a big fish in a big pond too, but this is the pond where my parents met, and it's a pretty darn good pond."

Caroll has been working at the same place for twenty-two years. Right after college he worked for a bit in the town where he went to college, but after he married his college sweetheart, they moved back to the town where he grew up in order to raise their own family.

"I know this town, and I knew I could be successful here," Caroll says about the reason for the return. "Besides, this is a great place to raise kids. I wanted my kids, three boys and a girl, to experience what I did, a town where everybody knows ya, and they're ready to knock some sense into ya."

Caroll points out that if it is a great place to raise kids then it has to be a great place to teach. "I like challenges, but I also like a game plan for success. I knew I could be successful here because I work hard and this town respects its teachers."

Caroll started his career as a social studies teacher, and that is still what he teaches. However, now he is the chair of the department. He also serves as the coach of a winning football team, on which one of his three sons plays, and he is the union president for the school district. He has power, and he likes it.

He also likes fighting for what he believes are noble goals and finds that the union position fulfills this need. It is somewhat surprising to learn that he is not interested in being an administrator. "I know what I do well, and that is what I choose to do. I want to fight with the kids, not their parents."

This is an important self observation; Caroll has a keen sense of what his skill set is, which is often the case with Competitors. Since winning is so important to them, they try their best to put themselves in situations where this is doable, if not inevitable.

This is not always easy for Competitors, depending upon their ability and courage to choose where they live. A competitor who is unable to secure a winning playing field at work quickly is discontented and may become combative or at least manipulative at home.

The context Caroll uses might also be familiar to a Competitor. He uses terms that invoke a sense of battle or gamesmanship. He is competitive, and his strategy is making sure he is playing a game that is winnable to him. He chose his town, career, and positions of power.

Caroll is gregarious and easy to talk to. People gravitate to him, even when they do not particularly like what he is doing or saying. In fact, Caroll intimidates many people, adults and children alike, but they will turn to him when they need help and advice, because he can get the job done. Caroll has spent most of his life striving to win, and since he is adept at choosing winnable games, he has indeed spent most of his life winning.

This in turn has built up his confidence and his ability to quickly assess a situation and the winning strategy. This is one of the main reasons people turn to him. He is successful and confident, and people like being around both of those characteristics. This even can become a bit of a self-fulfilling prophesy itself. People not only seek out successful people, but also invest in them. They invest their time, money, and support. This gives the Competitor tangible resources as well as a confidence boost.

Caroll needs to be careful that he does not come to expect from everyone this type of admiration. When Competitor-teachers start expecting others to be in awe of them, they not only can lose their focus on the game at hand, but also can alienate friends and relatives who stop feeling appreciated and instead feel used and exploited.

Competitors are generally self-absorbed. Although at times this can be charming or interesting in a charismatic person, that wears off quickly if you find yourself continuously in the company of someone who only is interested in advancing his or her own plot. Once aware of this downfall, the

Competitor-teacher can work on becoming less self-absorbed, or at least, as a tactic, decrease its appearance.

Caroll has worked out a dance with his wife, and they seem content together. She seems comfortable in a supporting position, and he makes sure to draw her out into the conversation when he sees her losing interest in the current conversation or activity. He is self-referent, but quickly picks up on the social cue of when interest wanes around him—at least by his loved one. A Competitor-teacher who strives to bring out the best in his students will need to develop a caring posture, if not a caring personality.

Caroll admits that there are plenty of people who do not admire him or seek to be in his shadow. He admits, however, that it hurts his feelings when he hears that people do not like him. "I'm really a softy, but I come across strong, and not everybody can handle that. But, there is nothing I can do about how people react to me. I wish all people would like me, but if they don't... oh well, that is their loss."

Most people are not likely to hear this vulnerable side of Caroll. And, many of the things that are important to Caroll put a barrier between him and them. Caroll drives one of the most expensive cars in town. It is his way of rewarding himself for a successful career, and it is his way of letting others know that he is successful. To him being successful in a career is measured, or at least demonstrated, mainly in income and prestige. While some of the town people admire his car, others are envious, and still others think of him as pretentious.

The same can be said about his house. While it is not one of the biggest in the town, it is on the lake, and it took many sacrifices for Caroll and his wife to afford it. His school office reflects the same concern for publicly establishing his success. Every degree, every bit of training, every win, every act of appreciation is displayed elegantly on a shelves on a wall in his office. Caroll wants to remind himself of his success, and he wants others to not just notice, but appreciate him. The best part of being on a winning team, Caroll might tell you, is acclaim and applause.

Caroll is well-liked by many of his school colleagues and a large number of his students—especially the athletes. This is in large part because Caroll is the football coach and that position alone brings respect in a small town where community identity can be created or enhanced by the performance of the football team.

You would not have to spend much time in the high school social studies classes that he teaches before you would be certain that he was a coach for something. Not only do the kids and teachers call him "Coach," but more noticeable is how he uses his coaching abilities to interact with his students. He indeed coaches them, and he loves doing it. However, the ones who do not respond well to game analogies, because they either do not understand them or they purpose-fully rebel against the image, find themselves disconnected from Caroll. And, it appears that Caroll does not care. His goal is to get them to behave and get the job done, and frankly, to do it better than anyone else has or could.

For the most part he is successful in getting his students up to the bar he has set for them. Unfortunately, these are high school students, and many of them would like to set the bar for themselves. Some of them would like more care and nurturing from him, but he truly does not believe that this is part of his job. Caroll has not yet figured this out, and when these kids do not succeed, he believes that he has somehow not gotten the message through to them. While he still ultimately blames them for their lack of interest and lack of learning, he grows frustrated.

There is room for growth here, but Competitors often miss opportunities for growth. They are the least reflective of the Stages because they focus much more on the future than on the past. Competitor-teachers would be wise to apply to their own lives the coaching techniques they use with others that build upon past mistakes.

Caroll enjoys his teaching and his coaching, but his main goal is to achieve what he believes is the ultimate success—to retire in a bigger house at the lake, with a nice boat, and a series of sunny days with which to entertain his friends and former colleagues.

Caroll is striving for a better lifestyle, but like so many Competitors, he often misses the wonderful aspects of his lifestyle right in front of him. His pattern of behavior is to be looking always for the next challenge, the next adventure, the next task to be accomplished. He also is more excited about what the lifestyle will say about him to his peers and the town's folks than he is about spending endless days relaxing with his wife and his friends.

The danger for Caroll and Competitor-teachers is focusing so much on the destination that the journey goes past unenjoyed—and when you think about it, life is a journey, not a destination. That is a long time to be think-ing about the future without appreciating the present. Caroll can continue to be a Competitor-teacher and learn how to find joy in the present, or he can move to the next stage where he will increase his influence, confidence, and day-to-day appreciation of life.

ARE YOU A COMPETITOR-TEACHER?

Do you find that you are proud of those aspects of yourself that are evident in Caroll—particularly the confidence? Do you find yourself chuckling as you note that the flipside of such confidence is riddled with battling others for control? Do you think it is a small price to pay for getting your way and enjoying life?

If so, you probably are a Competitor-teacher. Competitor-teachers are a confident and often gregarious bunch. They love their assets and are amused by their deficits. If you are one of them, you are very adept at choosing a winnable game, and when you win, your confidence spikes, thereby nudging you on to the next endeavor. You are motivated by winning and being able to show others the fruits of your successes, whether these are degrees, titles, trophies, or fancy cars.

Athletes and coaches are particularly comfortable as Competitor-teachers for the obvious reasons, but anyone with a heightened competitive spirit will find that he enjoys being a Competitor-teacher, at least for a time. Those who are not naturally competitive actually can learn helpful competitor skills when they are in this Stage—but they will not enjoy themselves nearly as much. That is because the Competitor-teacher is driven by the need to be better than others, and only if this is a natural attribute is this Stage in life particularly comfortable.

The competition in this Stage does not come about just as a result of a need for affirmation and validation, there also is a need to excel and achieve. This is the stage for testing one's endurance, learning to play fair, and developing coping skills for failure.

It is true that the Competitor-teacher's sights are too focused on comparisons to others, but the ability of the Competitor-teacher to draw inspiration and determination from this search for excellence should not be underestimated or underadmired. As a Competitor-teacher you can, and often do, achieve much, and in the meantime inspire others to do the same. The reason for you, the Competitor-teacher, to move to the next stage is for more balance and happiness in life and to find the deeper meaning of your individual existence.

As a Competitor-teacher, you are confident and tough-minded. You may already have noticed that even those who adamantly disagree with you seem to seek you out for a good debate, and administrators whom you have challenged may still come to you to find out what your opinion is. Of course, as a Competitor-teacher you still will find yourself on the outside of the tent more than you would really like.

You also probably know that even your closest relationships hang in the balance. You see the world as forced choices, and this includes your relationships. Things are good or bad, right or wrong, worth it or not. Your ability to walk away from a relationship is as strong as your ability to form lasting bonds. Your gifts are your demons, and you know that. You know it because of your gamesmanship and your ability to assess the strengths and weaknesses of those around you. You do the same to yourself.

As you develop through the Stages, you will find your tolerance for commitment to increase—particularly as it relates to acceptance and forgiveness. If you harness this, it can become the impetus for your movement to the next stage.

As a Competitor-teacher, you enjoy what you can learn from other people, and as you learn that your superficial view of others, often as pawns, stands in the way of our own growth and understanding, you will decide to buck up and risk any disadvantage that might come with opening yourself up to others. And, when a Competitor makes the decision that it is time to move to the next Stage, it happens very quickly. After all, you are as internally competitive as you are externally competitive—a Personal Best is as important as a win.

Your Strengths

You, the Competitor-teacher, are close to your base senses and you rely heavily on the earth and the gifts of the earth and the human body. This affinity with nature keeps you adventurous and a hands-on learner. This is the type of learning that you are most comfortable delivering to your students as well.

If you are a science teacher and a coach, you probably are a very happy Competitor-teacher and may even find sufficient justification to stay right where you are. Whatever your academic discipline is, your challenge throughout this book will be to discover that spirituality also is a discipline that you can better understand and master, and that other people have a significant role in what you can accomplish.

Competitor-teachers may be somewhat of "nature" lovers, but that should not be confused with being a lover of that which is natural and organic. Competitors appreciate human-made systems, organizations, and rules, and they fit well with strong hierarchical systems. As a matter of fact, it often is the Competitor-teachers among us who will create the hierarchical systems if they do not already exist.

While you have great strength of character and admirable coping skills, when you are at this Stage you can be combative and will often view things as polarized. Life is viewed from the same perspective as nature—conquerable. So, although you have the ability to carve out a nice kingdom in whatever position you hold, you still are limited in your perspective and what you can ultimately deliver to yourself and to those you care about.

This means that being right, good, and in control are extremely important to you, and so you will work hard to be righteous and to guide your students to do the same. Parents probably love this about you, as do administrators. As a matter of fact, many administrators are Competitor-teachers. But it is when they advance to other stages that their peers and subordinates start referring to them as leaders rather than as administrators.

Your Challenges

When the Competitor-teacher has taken the time to know the facts of the situation at hand, he can be a tireless advocate for a worthy cause. A good Competitor-teacher often is a successful teacher and role model. It is not a bad stage in which to hang out and build your resume. However, as a Competitor-teacher you could jump on an issue without due consideration. You are just as likely to spend your time and energy pushing for something that is half-baked. And as a Competitor, you will fight for this half-baked idea until everyone is dining on an undercooked meal.

Your Relationships

While the Competitor-teacher can be wonderfully successful and even inspirational to others in all Stages of development, the overconfidence that often is displayed by them is not always appreciated by other people.

Competitors may be admired enough that colleagues are quick to enjoy their wit, drive, and general enthusiasm for life, but the Competitor-teacher generally finds that he does not experience the depth of intimacy in relationships that he would like. As a Competitor-teacher, you may not even realize that most people are able to sense the manipulation and power-plays that you employ and keep relationships rather superficial. Even your intimate relationships can cool down and become perfunctory as partners seek emotional safety.

Competitor-teachers are very sexual. Sexuality is an important aspect of humans, so it should be a component of your life at any Stage, but Competitor-teachers need to be cautious that they do not use sex, or sexual partners, as a means to an end. Be careful that you are valuing yourself and others since exploitation could come disturbingly easy for you as you seek adventure and conquest. Enjoy the sensual aspects of yourself, but remember the importance of balance, safety, and kindness.

As mentioned earlier, as a Competitor-teacher, you continuously will see yourself in comparison with others, constantly asking yourself "who am I better than; who am I worse than?" This means that when you find people whom you view to be your equals, you likely will form quick alliances, and in time, these can develop into friendships.

However, whether conscious or not, your motivation in most alliances will be to advance a personal goal or need rather than to form a bond based on mutual needs or the needs of the other. This, of course, is the antithesis of friendship. You may not even take the time to hear what others need. If you do, you are likely to put them in a quid pro quo construct. Your loyalty within these alliances will be strong, and if they do develop into friendships they will become comfortable and habitual.

You enjoy being around other people who are active, and you particularly gravitate to athletes and adventurers. While you can learn from more passive types and enjoy the change of pace, it is more likely that your enduring relationships will be with people who are similar to you because Competitor-teachers prefer to be with people whose motives they understand and whose behaviors they can find predictable. That is part of your winning strategy. Your competitive spirit relies on regular validation, so you also like to be around people who appreciate your talents and abilities and are quick to tell you so.

Your World

Competitor-teachers like to be active and engaged in their environment. As a Competitor, your environment is another area where you seek to challenge yourself and gain control. You may even set-up challenges and opportunities to learn within your environment. You have clear ideas of what is right and wrong. Once you have decided what is right for you, you believe it is right for others as well. After all, you would not develop an opinion about something unless you already had decided that it was the right thing to do and the right opinion to have.

You tend to think that you, and those who think like you, have found the truth, and you are willing to both advocate and fight for your views. This also is how you view your religious beliefs. Unfortunately, you also see religion and spiritual issues as polarized as a sporting event, so those who think differently than you are easily labeled as wrong, and not winning the race to God. So, although you are a transmitter of justice, your justice does tend to be based on a less than well-balanced paradigm. If you are actively religious, which is likely the case if you are Competitor-teacher, you may see society the way Augustine (1225–1274 BCE) did, as caught up in a battle of good and evil.

As a Competitor-teacher you do understand that there are opinions different from yours, but you assume this is because those holding different beliefs just have not heard all of the facts. If you think the beliefs of others are infringing upon your environment, you will not hesitate to try to set them straight.

As mentioned earlier, you appreciate a strong hierarchy. In addition, you rely on empirical evidence to form and support your views and beliefs. You are quite certain that there is a correct or optimal answer to every question, and that everyone should be seeking it. This makes you a strong match for established religious traditions with entrenched dogma and well-developed doctrine. You are particularly comfortable in a belief system that acknowledges an all-knowing God who rewards and punishes behavior.

This all comes together to mean that you are not as aware as you could be of the different worldviews, and you may actually have a difficult time taking a different cultural perspective or empathizing with such. As a matter of fact, many Competitor-teachers find such terms as "worldview" and "cultural context" to be assaults against their belief systems and the very structures that have given rise to them.

As a Competitor-teacher seeking to grow and develop, you may want to take into consideration the words of author Peter Senge who tells us that "[s]tructures of which we are unaware hold us prisoner" (Senge, p. 94).

Your Approach to Teaching

You see education as necessary for a well-informed citizenry and well-run democracy. As part of this goal, you believe children need to be taught how to control and channel their energies, appetites, and bodies.

Helping students become disciplined is important to you, as you believe that a disciplined person is one who has optimal control over his life and therefore an enhanced ability to succeed. You are very encouraging of others to push themselves toward success, but you generally do not become emotionally invested in your students or their products.

However, you do like to see happiness in people, and you will seek opportunities for everyone to experience success, even though you believe that they need to take on the responsibility to translate the opportunity to reality.

Games and contests are most surely a part of your instruction, but you also appreciate student demonstrations as ways for students to show their competence, especially to each other. If you are an experienced teacher, you probably by now have integrated awards and incentives within your classroom.

You are most likely successful at using categorizing and sequencing in your learning environment, and when you test your students, you prefer to use forced choice opportunities. It is natural for you to work within a paradigm that sets one thing as better than, or more correct than, another.

If you do not already use the 3–2–1 strategy, you might want to. It is an instructional approach that asks the students first, the terms they learned, second, the ideas they learned, and third, the skills they mastered. It has the elements of a game, but the opportunity for you to assess student learning.

As a Competitor-teacher you like to have a learning environment that is orderly and organized. Just as there is a place for everything and a role for everyone at games and sporting events; you like to be so organized. You also like for everyone to participate. So, while you like to have rules that may inhibit some student exploration, your goal is to make sure that everyone has something to do.

Because of your concern with the overall picture and your competitive nature, you have a tendency to focus on the group and the group's goal. Students in your classroom have an opportunity to learn and nurture important collaborative and negotiating skills, but they also are at risk of having their individual needs and desires altogether missed.

You like to reward good behavior and achievement, but you will not hesitate to punish students who misbehave, and you need to be careful that you do not shame those who achieve below your expectations or their own abilities whether you are working with adults or children. It is true that your students have the opportunity to learn collaboration and negotiation from you, but there is a danger that they can learn to be overly competitive, if not combative. While it is not a bad thing to teach your students how to gain a competitive edge, you need to be careful that you are not pitting students against each other or making comparisons among them on an ongoing basis. Teaching moments can happen without one student feeling greater than and another feeling lesser. Remember that comparison is not the only model available for making a point.

From a curriculum standpoint, the Competitor-teacher is a traditionalist at heart. You are comfortable using from one year to the next what has worked. No sense breaking a winning streak, would be your basic argument. This strategy generally has worked well for you, but it has not worked for all of your students. Your students will be better served if you become familiar with various intelligences and learning styles and incorporate this individual approach to your design and use of curriculum. This is something you could become very good at because you are a strategist. You just need to strategize for a series of individual wins rather than for a large group win—think swim team rather than football team.

Your choice for developing your own curriculum would be to build upon specific outcomes. You might not feel comfortable referring to your approach as "outcome based" because of the lingering 1980s' connotations. You are however comfortable with a clear game plan based on specific goals and objectives. You also want to know ahead of time what is going to be measured. For the Competitor-teacher, using a backward design approach for curriculum development, such as Wiggins and McTighe's (1998) Understanding

By Design, will be very helpful in articulating goals and designing a method for getting there.

Moving from Competitor to Protector

Life as a Competitor-teacher is filled with clear ups and downs. As a Competitor-teacher your emotions often follow your successes and failures, and you tend to see most challenges in a black and white fashion. So, it is not uncommon for the Competitor to seem moody to others. This can be problematic for you if you do not recognize your own mood swings. You would avoid many conflicts if you were able to ascertain when people were reacting to your mood and your posture rather than to your words or your ideas. You tend to erroneously assume that it always is the latter.

Those closest to you understand your motivation and likely have adapted to your competitive nature. That means that their approach to you probably incorporates a level of gamesmanship. In that way, the people around you have taken a role in *your* dance, making it harder for you to move to the next Stage because you not only have to make changes to yourself, but also on some level you have to untangle yourself from others.

Although Competitor-teachers can operate at a frenetic pace and have mood swings, being a Competitor-teacher is not unpleasant. While there are ups and downs, you generally feel in control of your life, and when you do not, you easily find another goal to entice and motivate you. So, the Competitor-teacher generally feels alive and purposeful and able to pull himself out of negative moods.

It is time to move to the next Stage when you have grown tired of the ups and downs of the Competitor-teacher, when you find that you are no longer as motivated by competition and being best, when you are hoping for a more holistic and calm approach to life, when you want to deliver more authentic educational opportunities for your students, or when your competitive drive challenges you to advance yourself.

If you find that you are resistant to the idea of moving to a more spirituality advanced orientation, you might want to consider what is holding you back. Often times the Competitor is held back because of religious beliefs taken to be true simply because it is what he believes. That is typical of the Competitor-teacher. Because he tends to be passionate about his beliefs, it is easy for him to confuse this passion for self-evident truth: I believe it; therefore it is true.

If you find this to be the case with you, it might be helpful for you to consider the words of Jung who said that when you fight against something vigorously as immoral and sinful, you are most likely fighting the shadow side of yourself. Make sure to give yourself time to digest new ideas to see if they find a comfortable place in your psyche. Don't fight to fight, and don't fight change just because it is change.

You also may be fearful of walking away from an orientation to the world that has worked for you, even if you realize now that it is not the most beneficial for your entire being or for the students in your charge.

The Competitor-teacher is in a strong place to utilize the growth avenues that relationships present us. You are strategic and good at seeing the attributes and weaknesses of others. This knowledge can be parlayed into bringing each of your relationships into their most healthy state of being—a state that serves the spiritual growth of both parties.

Because of your ability to employ charisma, you can engage others and see how they are able to challenge your shadow side and help you overcome the combative aspects that stand in your way. It is through relationships that the Competitor-teacher will learn to temper his weaknesses and build his strengths.

One of the main things that a Competitor can do to enable movement to the next Stage is to look at his worldview—particularly how he views other people and their roles in his life. The Competitor tends to believe that life is not really fair. He does not rest assured in a balance in life, but instead believes that he has to "beat" others in order to be truly successful. This is based upon a belief that rewards are finite. Abolishing this belief is key to understanding the Competitor-teacher and moving on to becoming a Protector-teacher. This also is how the Competitor can avoid taking on a martyr role.

The Competitor makes most of his progress when he realizes that the important rewards in life are infinite: love, courage, admiration, respect, and yes, even money. There is enough to go around for everyone.

The Competitor-teacher also tends to believe that his independence will come at a cost, and so he is more comfortable being part of a team. This may seem confusing, because his over-confidence often looks like independence, but it is not, and he fears that independence is synonymous with confrontation, abandonment, and loss. An element of this is that he is not secure in the concept of unconditional love. In his core he still believes that he has to prove himself and be part of the family, group, school, company–whatever the team is.

This may not be something of which the Competitor is consciously aware. He feels that to pull away he will have to not just compete, but confront, and not just confront others, but also himself. This would cause change, and ultimately, he believes, it would cause to fall apart the familial and institutional systems that he has built up. This fear of loss and disconnect from the structure of his worldview is the basis for what keeps a Competitor-teacher in this Stage.

If you are a Competitor-teacher, try not to view things as polarized. You are not playing a zero sum game. Understand as Kierkegaard did that existence is the field of possibilities. Try to imagine and believe in all possibilities. Happiness is not found in the winning or in the losing, but in the playing of the game, or it cannot be found at all. Revisit the writings of Augustine as well, and instead of fully accepting his view of good versus evil, learn how he brought in history to develop his philosophy.

Do the same thing for yourself. Acquaint yourself with the development of philosophical and religious thinking in the context of history. You will more easily move to the next Stage if you are able to see how your thinking developed and to what it was in response.

Moving to the next Stage also means enjoying the journey. A focus on winning is a focus on the future. Once, when I was traveling in a foreign country with a group, I noticed the difference in how some of us walked from one location to another. There were a couple of people who quickly and sure-footedly weaved their way in and out of the crowds and arrived at the destination minutes—actually scores of minutes—ahead of others of us. But, later when we were recapping the day, it was clear what they had not noticed and enjoyed. They did not see the misspelled street sign; they did not notice the kids doing street acrobatics; they did not observe the heated argument between the octogenarians outside the market. Ask yourself where life happens. Is it at the destination, or is it on the journey?

Focus on being less self-absorbed. Remember that everyone is in his or her own game—most of the time we are not playing the same game even if we have mutual goals. In order to move to the next Stage, the Competitor-teacher needs to appreciate how to recognize mutual goals and form opportunities for collaboration with other teams. As a Competitor-teacher, resist the temptation to see collaboration the way a favorite colleague of mine liked to describe it: "unnatural act between consenting adults."

Incorporating the Right Changes

The Competitor-teacher generally stresses winning, so a good instructional strategy to employ while trying to become a Protector-teacher is Two Plus Two. Two Plus Two means offering your students two positive comments about their work along with two comments that point out areas that need improvement—some refer to this as the praise-and-criticism combo. When you use this strategy, end with the positive feedback in order to leave your students with optimum confidence and a sense of individuality.

You still will enjoy using incentives and rewards in your interactions with students, but consider either letting the students choose when they have earned them, or at least award students for knowledge and skills acquired even if it was not sufficient for your purposes or directly on point with your goals.

Creating a climate of optimism and enthusiasm will serve you well as you move to the state of Protector-teacher. Your gamesmanship attitude is something on which you can build a greater sense of community through fun activities. Take this time to focus, not just on games and contests, but on other activities that cause your students to relax, have fun, and laugh.

Because you are a strategist and good team builder, you will find success in professional groups, particularly advocacy groups. As you seek to improve your teaching through the use of this guide, you would be well-advised to find opportunities to explore this growth in activities that also seek to improve not just your own students, but more students through work for the greater good. You have the ability to reach out to a larger audience. Instead of thinking about collegial opportunities as a chance to get or keep ahead of your peers, think of them as opportunities to network and spread your gifts further.

Give special consideration to those professional development opportunities that will help you understand and utilize differentiated instruction so that you can continue your focus on your students as individuals.

Incorporating Spiritual Practices

Below are Stage-specific practices designed to do two things: they will honor and celebrate the Stage you are at, and they will prepare you for the expectations of the next Stage. While it is your goal to develop into more advanced Stages, this will happen more quickly if you express understanding and gratitude for the Stage in which you currently find yourself. Full appreciation for the wonderful person you already have become is necessary for spiritual growth.

Competitor-teacher Prayer

> *Thank you for the abundance that you have brought into my life.*
> *Help others to find all they need in life*
> *and the courage to seek more.*
> *Bless me with the ability to always appreciate*
> *the gifts you have given me and my family,*
> *and for that matter to appreciate my family more.*
> *Bless me with the ability to comprehend and appreciate my own value,*
> *especially my value to my students*
> *as I so often believe that I do not do enough.*
> *Guide my steps as I seek a happier and healthier lifestyle, and*
> *as I seek to be a champion for what is right and good.*
> *I have much strength and fortitude.*

Keep me healthy and happy
and walking a path that is good and righteous,
and help me be the best teacher I can be.

Competitor-teacher Meditations

You will need to read through this entire meditation before you begin. If you are able, do this meditation outdoors near running water. If you are not able to, it would be nice to have the sound of water next to you indoors—even a small desk fountain.

Sit in whatever position is comfortable. Spend a couple of minutes with your mind blank. See what thoughts come to you. To begin your Competitor-teacher meditation, close your eyes and picture a bright orange light in your mind.

Picture yourself feeling no emotions. Think of a time that you were content—but not necessarily happy. Find a period of time when emotions were not controlling your thoughts or your actions. Now, take that feeling—that feeling of being in your body, but not ruled by your body and picture yourself in water swimming and floating freely. See the water. It is the most beautiful blue color you ever have seen. Feel the coolness of the water. Feel it touching every part of your body. It is refreshing and cleansing. Your body tingles, and you feel childlike and playful. You feel peaceful.

Think of this water as your emotions—all of your emotions mixed together. Do you see how the negative and positive are equally neutral to your body? Do you see that this water could only be positive or negative if you named it so?

Think about how you can use this metaphor of water to neutralize emotions when they wash over you. Think about how you can rename the emotion, because it was neutral until you named it. Think about how you can choose to immerge from it when you want. Think about how you can dry it off. Spend a couple of minutes thinking about how blessed you are to have emotions, but be able to control them. Be thankful that you are learning that you are in control of your emotions, they are not in control of you—you can walk away from them when you need to and wash them off when you need to.

Competitor-teacher Journaling

Make a list of your successes over the past twelve months. Now rewrite those successes with a sentence next to them explaining why you are proud of yourself.

Make a list of your failures over the past twelve months. Now rewrite those failures with a sentence stating what you learned from the experience. Next to what you have learned, write the words "The experience is over. I have toweled away the negative feelings I had associated with it."

Competitor-teacher Movements

Swimming and water activities will serve the Competitor-teacher. Find opportunities to be active in water, either playing or swimming. If this proves difficult, then make it a point to take long baths. Other activities that will help you are those that have a fluid motion to them, such as rowing, Hula-Hooping and belly dancing.

Competitor-teacher Music

The Competitor-teacher should listen to music with a lot of rhythm such as Latin or Reggae. The following artists are recommended:

David Bisbal
Chayanne
Poncho Sanchez
Gipsy Kings

The Competitor-teacher is summarized in the table below:

Table 2.1

View of self	Deserving of success
Motivation	To be better than others
Strengths	Problem solving; coaching
Weaknesses	Ego driven; sees things polarized; combative
View of others	As rivals or pawns
View of God, spirituality	God is watching and keeping track of good and bad behavior. God can be vengeful; behavior on behalf of God is justified; other religions are wrong—probably evil. Having affirmations that one's beliefs are accurate is most important.
View of education	Give a competitive edge
Instructional strategies	Games; examples
Classroom management	Through rewards and incentives
Use of curriculum	Workforce development; structured
Necessary to move a stage	Realize that things are not true and correct just because you believe them

Stage 3

The Protector

Therefore sages keep their faith and do not pressure others. So the virtuous see to their promises, while the virtueless look after precedents. The Way of heaven is impersonal; it is always with good people.

—Lao Tzu, Tao Te Ching

RAMON

Ramon sits contently in his classroom waiting for a kid to pop in with a question. Someone always comes by to speak with Ramon after school. That is why he makes sure to stay late in his office rather than join his colleagues in the lounge or on the highway home.

When asked why he does not go join the other teachers at least for a little while, Ramon responds "They don't need me." Ramon underestimates the benefits of collegial relationships. He does not spend enough time with his peers to realize how much he could learn from them about teaching and about content. He is so focused on his own goals for his students that he does not take the time for personal growth—growth that could help him better reach his students.

Ramon's colleagues like him because he is a kind man who clearly is dedicated to his students. But they know that they really do not know him, and they know that he does not reach out to them. This does not enable trust to grow between Ramon and the other teachers, and as such, when Ramon is fighting for something he believes in or seeking help to a problem, the other teachers are not quick to rally behind him.

Ramon likes to care for others and thrives on feeling needed. Ramon is very happy working at this inner-city community college, and he especially likes the atmosphere he has created in his classroom—an atmosphere that he believes is welcoming and nurturing.

While he is fiercely protective of his students and their feelings, he does not mollycoddle them. He allows them to feel frustration, aggravation, and even temporary loss of esteem. He knows that life can be hard, and he is looking at helping create in them skills that will guide and support them throughout their lives. He understands that a little pain now can prevent a lot of pain later.

While he is competent in group instruction, Ramon prefers small groups or one-on-one tutoring. And, he divides up his instruction to maximize strategies that best work in those configurations. He wants to prepare his students for the real world, and he believes he can best do this by knowing them well. Ramon also enjoys getting to know himself well, and so he likes being alone to contemplate his next lesson or activity. Even now, he enjoys sitting in solitude waiting for the first young scholar to visit.

Teaching is a new field for Ramon—two years completed, to be exact. He used to be a nurse, but he came to believe that most of the problems he dealt with as a nurse could have been prevented if both he and his patients knew more. So for years he contemplated changing fields. He knew he wanted to be a teacher, but change is hard for Ramon, so he spent another ten years as a nurse wanting to be a teacher. One of the reasons change is hard for Ramon is because he is a "Protector."

Protectors are caregivers, and they feel most competent as caregivers when they can keep as much as possible the same. They tend to be conservative in all aspects of their lives. They can protect themselves and the people they love more easily if the challenges and threats remain relatively the same. The changing of environments means having to relearn risks and the associated foils. It is in the transition from one environment to another that Protector-teachers feel most vulnerable.

During the last four years of his nursing career, Ramon pursued an M.A. in education. He eagerly soaked up knowledge with the intent of being the best teacher he could. He also was quite ready to live the lifestyle of a teacher, summers off, isolated classroom, academic discretion—and he was quick to tell his friends this. But most of all Ramon was looking forward to making a difference in the lives of new nurses and ultimately their patients.

He wanted to share with them everything that he had learned throughout his life in the hopes of making their lives easier, now and in the future. "I hope Ramon realizes that he can't teach them everything about life," his friend Altea chuckled. "I also hope he realizes that their lives are not all the same." This last observation of Altea's is an important one. Because Protector-teachers are conservative, they tend to apply the same solution across situations.

Even the Protector-teacher who knows each student as an individual will often expect little deviation among the various personalities when it comes to their learning behavior. This can lead to disappointment for the Protector-teacher as he watches his well-intended plans reap unpredictable results. But, Ramon worked through his fears, and grew enough to take the big step of changing careers and becoming a teacher.

The first year of teaching was wonderful for Ramon, and his wife shared in the excitement. His wife Julie had been a dental receptionist for thirteen years, and she never had to take work home. During his first year of teaching, she gave Ramon a lot of help in the evenings, and he loved it. The two of them would scour books and the Internet for just the right resources to bring into the classroom.

The second year of teaching brought a change in their household. Ramon had not lost any of his enthusiasm for the job, but Julie had. She was no longer happy that Ramon spent so much of his time at school. She felt that the job was coming between them. She would complain that as a nurse he never brought work home, and he had to remind her of the night and weekend shifts early in his nursing career. But, Julie felt neglected, and she believed their two middle-school kids were neglected too. She missed the time they all had together in the evenings and weekends. "I know this has been hard on Julie. She claims that she is no longer my favorite project. I love her deeply, but I have to help people who need my help. I have to have a project . . . or several." Ramon goes on to explain that this is a continuous cycle in their marriage. "I need to be needed—but after all of these years of marriage, she really doesn't need me as much. I guess that causes me to spend more time at school where I can see my influence."

Yes, Ramon spends a great deal more time at school. He even set up a nursing club. He and another instructor arranged to spend an hour or two each Saturday answering questions, coaching, and facilitating discussions.

This is a common pattern for Protector-teachers: to put their students ahead of their families. It is not intentional, but it is not entirely unintentional. Ramon speaks with great pride about his family: "I have a great family. Everyone is happy, and the kids are doing great in school." But, he understands enough about himself to add the following: "Sure, Julie and the kids complain that I am not around as much as they would like. But they understand. They know how much these young adults need me, and they are proud of the work I do."

Protector-teachers know what they need to do to help particular students, and they will go that extra mile, the way Ramon did when he set up the nursing club. What they do not realize is to what extent it takes emotional energy and additional time away from themselves and their families. Because they have big hearts, and their primary intention in life is to care for others, they often ignore the results of their actions in favor of their motives. In other words, they mean well and truly have trouble understanding when others point out that they have fallen short.

Protector-teachers believe good intentions are sufficient. The negative aspect of this is that they do not easily notice or understand when someone they are caring for feels neglected. This often is a huge frustration for Protector-teachers: they do not feel appreciated by the people closest to them, and it usually remains an elusive goal.

Ramon is more insightful than many Protector-teachers. He seems quite skilled at understanding what his wife is feeling, even if he is not ready to make the changes she is requesting. In turn, his wife is still frustrated, but she feels listened to and understood. This is a skill that Ramon will want to build upon as he seeks to move to the next Stage of spiritual development.

Ramon can continue to be a Protector-teacher and learn how to balance his time and affection, or he can move to the next Stage and operate at a level of unconditional love thereby bringing more harmony and happiness to all aspects, and all people, of his life.

ARE YOU A PROTECTOR-TEACHER?

Do you spend most of your time taking care of other people, including other adults? Do you do this, for the most part, without any expectation of appreciation, and yet find at times that you resent the lack of reciprocity? Do you constantly hear from colleagues, neighbors, and associates what an amazing capacity you have for nurturing and caring for others? Do you feel complete when you are serving others, and find yourself restless and even in a dark mood when there is no one who really needs you at the moment?

If these scenarios sound familiar to you, you probably are a Protector-teacher. It is the balance between the negative and positive aspects of caring that defines this Stage. Many teachers are comfortable in the Protector-teacher role. As a matter of fact, we probably would find that most teachers, especially elementary teachers, are in this Stage. This is a role that is notable for its one-sidedness. The Protector-teacher gives more than he perceives he gets, but what is most important about this fact is that the Protector-teacher is getting exactly what he seeks.

Three things tend to happen to a Protector-teacher: he does not actively seek nurturing; he does not notice when he does get nurturing; and through his divided attention, he tends to drive away many people who would be willing to nurture him.

You see, Protector-teachers are adept at giving, but they are not as skilled at receiving. That is why it can become a natural place for teachers, but not necessarily the most comfortable. This is because such a selfless orientation for teachers is compatible with our societal views and expectations of teachers: Our teachers cannot and should not expect nurturing from their students. In addition, teachers do not have enough contact with their colleagues, and too often their administrators step into authoritarian rather than inspirational roles.

The act of caring is intricately woven with power. Even if your motives are honorable, when you care for someone you either take their power or neutralize it. When you seek care from someone, you often subordinate your power to your current need for attention and nurturing. Protector-teachers are driven by this type of power. They want to protect others, but their motivation to do so is based on control more than it is based on love and compassion. That does not mean that they do not love people, it just means that they operate from a base of power, which *can* occlude love. Caregiving in our society is not as reciprocal as it should be.

The Protector-teacher can be adept as either a warrior or a servant. These are the two primary ways of protection, and both of these aspects can be negative or positive. A warrior can fight for what is right and for the benefit of others, but a warrior also has within him the tendency to fight for the sake of the fight. The same can be true about the servant side of a Protector-teacher. He can serve a good cause, or he can become obsequious and acquiesce to people and projects that are not noble. Both can be good if balanced together and if the focus of protection is the students.

As a Protector-teacher, you generally are quite content with your life. You do not believe that you have to prove yourself, but it still is important to you to do so because you enjoy approval, and depending upon your home life growing up, you may actually need such validation. You also know that by proving yourself, you increase your chances of being involved in the protection of what you hold dear, whether it is a class schedule, a curriculum, or a text. For that reason, you as a Protector must guard against complacency and laziness; it could quickly lead to a depressed state of mind.

Sometimes it is difficult to get you motivated to do something if you do not see the direct relationship it has to those you are seeking to protect, serve, or nurture. Similarly, you resist protecting those you do not deem worthy. Guard against this type of selfishness, as there are many who could benefit from your care, and your judgment of them gets in the way of that. Keep in mind that there is much for you to contribute and much for you to learn through involvement in things that do not particularly hold your interest.

Start taking risks that could benefit your growth. Your belief system is rather conservative, as are your actions, so you also do not take well to sudden change. As a matter of fact, on a good day unexpected change can annoy you and on a bad day it can send you into a panic as you feel your skill set drifting away. You need to have more faith in your abilities. Your skills can be transferred and you can make a difference as you grow.

Your contentment in life does enable you to see the best in those around you, for the most part. You truly are an optimist. But, you will need to regularly ask yourself whether the contentment you feel is sufficient for your life, or whether there is a reason to grow and learn more. After reading the rest of this book, I think you will see that there are some benefits to building upon what you already have and taking the risk of moving and changing.

Your Strengths

As a Protector-teacher, you are not just a loving and nurturing person, you also are extremely responsible—particularly when you are motivated and fully engaged. If you agree to an assignment, it will be done, and it will be done well and on time.

You tend to be overly optimistic in time management too, so it is not uncommon for you to take on a great deal of responsibility. You may volunteer for many activities or accept more tasks than you are easily capable of doing. You will then sacrifice something else to keep this promise—maybe family time, maybe sleep—but it likely will be something invisible to those whom you are trying to impress.

While you are responsible, you do not do a terrific job of keeping promises, even though you believe that keeping promises is important. This is an area of weakness, but that probably is because you do not view it as a dimension of responsibility. You view promise-keeping more as a moral decision and context specific. You tend to suffer from what I call promise-recency—the ability to only keep your recent promises. You are more apt to keep the most recent promises made and neglect or ignore the more distant ones that you have made. You also will make promise-keeping decisions based on a risk-reward analysis rather than a credibility-reciprocity analysis. This is all because your view of protection is to care for what needs immediate attention.

Your Challenges

Your challenge throughout this book is to understand that, because you are a Protector and a caregiver, people give you power over themselves and what they love. While you generally are motivated by good intentions, you are only human. You are capable of abusing this power if you are not careful.

One of the reasons that your loved ones become jealous and resentful of other aspects of your life, is not just because they miss you and miss your attention, but also because they have given you power over themselves. It is very scary when one gives someone power over himself only to find that the party in question is not attentive. It also is true that loved ones and colleagues can become resentful of you because they think you might be abusing the power they have given you. The way you can abuse this power is by putting conditions on your attention and caregiving; by not keeping your promises; by not giving the gift of time.

Your Relationships

Protector-teachers seemingly have an enormous capacity for love and nurturing due in large part to the depths of their commitment and loyalty. They are also adept at determining and delivering the responses people seek. This is a strength on which to build, and you would be wise to always find out directly from your friends and loved ones what they need from you and whether you are delivering.

You get along well with other people, but you prefer to be in relationships where power is in play and you have the ability to harness and use it. This is one of the reasons this Stage works for you. Your relationships generally are based on a quid pro quo. You might give more than you get, but you are not willing to give if you will not get something back, at least at some point. With your students, the "something" most likely is their respect and obedience.

You like to be with people who either understand this intuitively, or operate from the same mode. Equality in relationships is important to you, and if you are protecting someone, you expect to similarly be protected by them in a different setting or situation. So whether conscious or not, you are likely seeking to be in relationships that are going to fulfill that need.

Protectors also tend to underestimate how much their own family and friends need them. This is because it is something they cannot let themselves know. There are not enough hours in the day for the loyal Protector-teacher to nurture and protect all of those in his or her care. So, when the Protector-teacher is focused on one person or group of people, others often feel the absence.

Of course the objects of their attention feel quite cared for. Since students are not looking for relationships longer than a school year or two, Protector-teachers are successful in reaching and motivating their students through interpersonal relationships and engagement, but there is a danger that this will come at the expense of their relationships with their spouse, children, and friends.

For the most part, you have good relationships with your colleagues especially those who work with you day in and day out and really know you and your heart. But you need to spend more time with them to develop trust.

Because of the strong roots you establish within groups and your own ability to set a tone or keep order within the group, you develop a strong sense of worth when you are with others. Your colleagues often will see and admire this, but they may also resent that they know you better than you know them.

As a Protector-teacher, you tend to be content and comfortable, which means you like the status quo and can become frustrated with those who do not seem to value it or the contributions of those acting within the "system." As a dear colleague of mine use to say when charged to think outside the box, "The box gets a bad rap."

Like my colleague, the Protector-teacher tends to see the goodness in himself and around him and wants to preserve it. You like the box you are in. When you do see things that are wrong—and of course you will—you mainly will view the problem as something from the outside trying to come in, and you will be quick to react to preserve what you have. This optimism and gratitude is valuable to spiritual development and should be maintained as you learn to better embrace change.

You also value cultural and historical context, so you view people in relationship to their surroundings and their backgrounds. You may make snap judgments and stereotype people, but it also is true that you try very hard to understand the other person's reality and how he or she came to have the perspectives he or she does. You believe that everything is explainable and even defensible based on history and context.

Your World

As a Protector-teacher, you can enjoy either being isolated or working with other people, but your nature causes you to easily subscribe to group thinking. Your sense of loyalty, along with your sense of protectionism, causes you to enjoy belonging to various groups. You tend to not be particularly active in these groups, unless they are advocacy groups, but you enjoy the security you get from knowing you are a member. Because the security is important to you, you quickly adapt the thinking of the group in order to ensure that you continue to fit in.

You view the world as linear and always developing. You believe that we and the societies we create are products, not only of *our* time and space, but also of the time and space that came before us. So you are not just a protector of individuals, but also of groups and their histories.

As you seek to better understand yourself, you first try to better understand the world, and you do this by looking at issues of time and space—history and geography. This gives you the parameters to make sense of your world. So, your worldview is concrete rather than intuitive, and it is based on what you have pieced together rather than on what others have told you to believe. You are a constructivist.

This constructivist orientation of yours causes you to be rigid in your religious beliefs, because you almost feel destined to believe what you do. If you are active in a faith community you are viewed by others in your community as a wonderful transmitter of structure and preserver of religious beliefs. Be careful though, because your need for order could cause you to be Machiavellian in your behavior. And, the strength and security you gain from dogma can be a barrier between you and those who could benefit from your wise counsel and protection.

If you are not part of a faith community, you probably are an adamant nonbeliever. You no doubt came to your decision to avoid traditional religion based on sociological analysis. Therefore, you are as zealous of a nonbeliever as other Protector-teachers are believers. You might even find yourself believing Marx's famous quote: "Religion is the sigh of the oppressed creature, the heart of a heartless world, just as it is the spirit of an unspiritual situation. It is the opiate of the people."

If you choose to advance to other Stages, you will discover more interesting nuances in the dance humanity has with religion. You will see that religious views are not easily categorized and judged.

Your Approach to Teaching

When you are charged with watching over the instruction of others, you are extraordinary in your care and vigilance. Teaching is a wonderfully fulfilling profession for a Protector. The Protector-teacher views education as a means to transmit culture, but in a way that is simultaneously insulating and readying. In other words, as a Protector-teacher, you are adept at balancing between preparing students for the real world and what it holds, while providing enough insulation and nurturing to provide a safe and supportive environment.

In your classroom you like to build upon knowledge and skill, so preparing and ensuring a foundation is very important to you. You do best when you are making sure that there is a scope and sequence and that your teaching is aligned to it.

Your students are likely to have the basics down pat, but there is some risk that you are not open to general inquiry from them. It is important that you remember that there are several ways in which a student can arrive at the correct answer to a problem or situation and that you do not have to be emotionally invested in their path, just their destination. Then, you have to be ready to incorporate new student paths into your scope and sequence.

You believe that your students are able to pull together knowledge by sharing views and arguing points. Using agreement circles would be a successful instructional strategy in your classroom as would paired problem solving. You also would enjoy being part of educational activities from fairs to seminars, because you would especially value the opportunity for students to showcase to each other what they have discovered and found particular value in.

Because you appreciate the historical context of knowledge and values, you would particularly enjoy taking your students on field trips or practica—something that most students also enjoy because of the active involvement they employ as well as the opportunities for individual meaning. The tone you set in your classroom is very respectful. It likely is traditional, and it will feel very warm and nurturing to those students who come from similarly traditional homes.

It would serve your students well if you continued to learn about the various backgrounds of your students so that you could ensure that you are honoring and preserving what is known and treasured by them as well. This is a gift you are currently ready to provide. If you work with young children you should make sure to actively engage their parents. Protector-teachers work well with parents and can bring out the best in them.

Students in your classroom generally are well-behaved because they understand the climate of respect that you are trying to instill. You treat them well, and as a result, they treat each other well—for the most part. Since your own optimism and work ethic cause you to pull away from your students at times, it is imperative that you set a tone of trust early and let them know that their education and care are your priority, even if you do not have all of the time to give them that you and they would both like to see. This type of upfront honesty will save you later on when you become overwhelmed with work and responsibility.

Children do well in the tutelage of a Protector-teacher, as long as the Protector-teacher is careful to not impose too much rigidity while also insulating them. Too much insulating can be, of course, very stifling for children. From a developmental standpoint, it would be correct to assume that a Protector-teacher is helpful to the development of young children who need to be protected while simultaneously guided. But, you need to be more careful when you are working with older students and adults who need less protection and more freedom.

When it comes to curriculum design, you are going to be most comfortable using well-defined competencies that are SMART: specific, measurable, achievable, relevant, and time-bound. It will be clear to you and your students just what is supposed to be learned and how your students will demonstrate that it has been learned.

If you have not done so already, you also will be particularly successful developing and using well-aligned rubrics in order to properly assess student mastery and progress toward mastery. This is natural for you, so consider utilizing and sharing this skill.

Moving from Protector to Mentor

You are a person of great honor and integrity. It is from this base that you will build the attributes necessary to move to the next Stage. You mainly need to work on a deeper and more complete understanding of yourself and what it is you are trying to protect and why. If you learn your own unconscious self, you will not project repressed elements of it onto other people (Jung).

Status quo is of utmost importance to you. Sometimes this is a good thing—such as when the status quo is providing you and your students with the success you seek. However, often you cling to what is valued because you are fearful that it will go away. This is a tendency that many conservative people have—to make decisions out of fear or loss. After all, the root of the word conservative is "conserve," which is to protect and maintain. It is a reactionary stance often to an unknown force that you believe will take away what you cherish.

You may understand the benefits of conquering your fears and growing your talents, but you also are content with how your life is working and unwilling to take a chance on the unknown. Protector-teachers may be quick to fight for or serve a cause, but they are not quick to disrupt what they have or what they are doing for a belief in something better.

Instead of fearing the hypothetical, you should try to operate more on faith in yourself, others, and a higher power. Because you can be so attentive and protective of others, you are not going to easily find support to move to the next Stage. As you seek to develop yourself, you might find that those closest to you are happy with you just the way you are. There are benefits to them to keep you at the Protector Stage.

You need to be confident that the Creator-teacher has equal abilities, although manifested differently, to care and protect those close to him. While you may not get a lot of support from others, it is through your belief in others that you will find the best inspiration and strength for moving to the next Stage. Like Hume (1711–1776), you truly believe that we each have a natural capacity for compassion. However, unlike Hume, you might be hanging on to the belief that reason alone can determine how you ought to act toward others.

At this point, you would benefit most from truly observing and reflecting upon your feelings and noting how it is through them that you really determine what the noble, moral, and ethical way is to behave toward others. Your goal at this point is to strengthen your ability to love, which begins with your ability to empathize and offer compassion. Take the time to listen to those you care about. Understand their lives, pains, passions, and dreams.

Your success at understanding and reacting to others is significant in the increasing development of your own intuition and personal empowerment. Take care not to use this skill to manipulate others. When you attempt to care for and nurture others, you touch their hearts.

You are ready to move on to the next Stage when you fully recognize this and ensure that those you are caring for set the context for your caregiving and when you are motivated by the strength of others rather than by their weaknesses.

As you seek to grow and develop, work on your ability to trust others and be open in turn to their ability to nurture and protect. It is wonderful to care for others, but you need to learn to open yourself up to being cared for as well. Be willing to take the risk of being vulnerable. Draw upon the Competitor-teacher's tolerance of the pain that comes with defeat.

The Protector-teacher seeks to understand the plight of others and how he can help. In order to move to the next Stage, the Protector-teacher needs to develop the type of compassion that arises out of detachment. Instead of seeing your place in the lives of others and how you can change their lives, seek to understand their perspective, especially their struggles and their pain. This needs to be seen on the individual level, not on the group level.

Then respect, admire, maybe even love them because of who they are, not because you can somehow help or change them. As Bonhoeffer advised "regard people less in light of what they do or omit to do, and more in the light of what they suffer" (Bonhoeffer, p. 468). Believe that you have the freedom to make choices, and believe that there is something better than what you have and you can achieve it.

You will most easily move to the next Stage, when you can see what needs to be protected for each individual student and how that can seem to be an attack on the status quo from someone else's perspective. Using the strength you receive from groups and a sense of belonging will help you move along to the next Stage. This is the time for you to become active with the groups in which you belong. Formal religion could really play a part in your advancement. But, you must draw yourself to the aspects of formal religion that celebrate the gifts of all people rather than of a few.

It is the time to develop your self confidence, but not at the expense of your view of others, rather because of your view of others. In other words, this is the time for you to realize the commonality among different people and to apply this to your personal power and what you can do on behalf of groups of people or all people rather than on those with whom you have taken a liking or who share the same belief system as you.

Incorporating the Right Changes

As you grow spiritually, you will want to focus on building the confidence of your students so they are less dependent upon you for motivation. You want to help them gain an internal locus of control. You then want to parlay that into guiding them into how to make effective choices for themselves.

There are several ways you can accomplish this. In addition to using yourself as a role model, you can have your students work with those from upper grades so that they can learn and utilize skills in a more incremental way. And then, you can make sure they spend time in collaborative activities and peer supported activities so that they gain comfort utilizing new skills in a more relaxed fashion. You can accentuate the need for follow-through so that students can develop discipline.

As your students develop their confidence and discipline and start moving away from you as their means of support and motivation, it is helpful to engage them in service-learning projects. This enables them to move back and forth between intrinsic and extrinsic motivation while focusing on the needs of others.

Seek professional development opportunities that can teach you how to be more creative and bring more creativity out of your students. Look into ways to use the arts to deliver your lessons or make them come alive.

Since you have a tendency to get into ruts, make an effort to become acquainted with the current research and best practices that pertain to instruction in general and your discipline in particular. You are confident and independent, and as such, you often feel that group learning is ineffective for you. You prefer self-paced individualized learning—probably even online learning. While these preferred methods are ones you should gravitate to, it also is true that you could benefit from professional development opportunities where you can hear and see the reaction your colleagues have to information. This is because you learn from what is taught, but you also learn from what you observe others taking away from a situation.

Incorporating Spiritual Practices

Below are Stage-specific practices designed to do two things: they will honor and celebrate the Stage you are at, and they will prepare you for the expectations of the next Stage. While it is your goal to develop into more advanced Stages, this will happen more quickly if you express understanding and gratitude for the Stage in which you currently are. Full appreciation for the wonderful person you already have become is necessary for spiritual growth.

Protector-teacher Prayer

> *Thank you for all of the goodness in the world*
> *and for the skills and knowledge you give to so many people*
> *in order to keep this complex world functioning.*
> *Help those who are not able to find the sustenance*
> *and shelter they need,*
> *and help us each find a way to make a difference with the less fortunate.*
> *Guide me as I seek to make the world a better place for others,*
> *and give me the ability to protect and guide my students*
> *in the best way possible.*
> *Bless me with the ability to use my optimism and kindness*
> *in ways that can guide other people.*
> *Bless me with the strength of confidence to face each day*
> *as a warrior fighting on behalf of others.*

Protector-teacher Meditation

You will need to read through this entire meditation before you begin. Sit as comfortably as you can. Spend a couple of minutes with your mind blank. See what thoughts come to you. To begin your Protector-teacher meditation, close your eyes and picture a bright yellow light in your mind.

Picture yourself as fire. Picture yourself traveling across a meadow and forest burning everything in sight. What do you feel?

Now picture yourself as intelligent fire. Imagine all of the animals gathered in one place, and as fire, you encircle them, but you do not harm or kill them.

Now, imagine that you do not destroy everything in your path, but instead you burn what needs to be replaced with fertile soil and you spare that which needs to provide food and shelter for people and animals. How do you feel?

Imagine yourself feeling satisfied with what you have done and unified with a great cause. Feel the great power of fire, but feel the more significant power of creating zones of protection and zones of creation.

Now, imagine this fire becoming smaller and smaller until it is a campfire in front of you. Look at the beautiful colors; feel the heat; smell the smoke. Imagine the fire moving to within your body. Feel the intelligent power you hold within you.

Protector-teacher Journaling

Make a list of people and situations that are confusing you and frustrating you right now.

Determine what is common among them. This could be the emotion they elicit, the behavior that is demonstrated, or the consequence that is brought about.

Write these things down. By looking at these common elements, determine what need or needs of yours are not being met. Now write a list of ways that you can easily and realistically meet those needs without connecting to those earlier situations or people.

Protector-teacher Movements

Competitive sports are rewarding and uplifting to the Protector-teacher, as is any type of strength training, particularly weight lifting. Concentrate on strengthening the body by integrating your muscles.

Protector-teacher Music

The Protector-teacher should listen to brass and brass ensembles. Find music that has strong, loud, slow beats—even marches. Some suggested artists are the following:

Canadian Brass
Philip Jones Brass Ensemble
Miles Davis
Feeling Brass Quintet

The Protector-teacher is summarized in the following table.

Table 3.1

View of self	Caring
Motivation	To make life better for others
Strengths	Optimistic; kind
Weaknesses	Overly protective; fearful of change; rigid
View of others	As less successful; as needing help
View of God, spirituality	God is forgiving; redemption is a goal; God is a regretful disciplinarian; beliefs should not evolve, nor should religion. Charity work and service is an important goal of religion. Finding ways to take care of less fortunate people is most important.
View of education	Transmit structure; insulate and prepare
Instructional strategies	Collaboration; group activities
Classroom management	Through signs and symbols
Use of curriculum	Give a real picture of life; understand social structure
Necessary to move a stage	Realize it is better to understand others than to control them

Stage 4

The Mentor

Waking up this morning I smile. Twenty four brand new hours are before me. I vow to live fully in each moment And to look at all beings with eyes of compassion.

—Thich Nhat Hanh

CHAD

When asked why he chose to be a teacher, Chad laughs and says "I think teaching chose me." Chad is a young principal at a large suburban high school. He cannot remember when he did not want to be a teacher. "It probably goes back to Mr. Williams. He was my third grade teacher, and I thought he walked on water. He told me 'Chad Johnson, you can be anything you want to be. You can achieve great things.' I will never forget how I felt when he said this to me. I felt excited and queasy. It was as if I stood on a bridge ready to bungee jump. And, with Mr. Williams there to support me, I took the jump. I guess it was a psychological jump into self-confidence. But, on another level, I think it was a jump into teaching. I think I decided then and there that I wanted to be another Mr. Williams."

It is not uncommon to find that Mentor-teachers were indeed touched by a mentor. There seems to be something about the act of personally reaching out to someone that becomes contagious.

Chad explains that "to this day I am inspired by Mr. Williams's belief in me from way back. I want to do the same for the kids in my school—at least the ones I can get to. I want them to know in their darkest moments that there is

63

someone out there rooting for them—someone who really cares about them."
He quickly adds, "but it's not about me—it doesn't have to be me."

Chad is right, and he is sincere. Mentor-teachers want their students to be
motivated by love and compassion and by a greater good. They believe that
this is best inspired by another person, and they are ready to hold that role.
They do not, however, think that they are alone in being able to mentor. They
believe that many people are suited, or can become suited, to mentor. As a
matter of fact, many Mentor-teachers go on to mentor not just students, but
other teachers, and they do this with the purpose of producing more like-
minded teachers—teachers ready to take on the cloak of mentor.

Mentor-teachers are highly motivated by human potential and how people
can bring out the best in each other. That is not to say that all Mentor-teachers
refer to themselves thusly. In some schools and school districts, the term
mentor has a concrete meaning, and maybe even a defined role. Therefore,
particular teachers may be Mentor-teachers, but they may not describe themselves that way if they have not held an actual "mentor" position.

You easily can spot a Mentor-teacher though, because they operate from an
orientation of abundance. They do not believe that they are competing with others for scarce resources. They believe that everyone will have what he or she
needs, and that somehow the universe will respond with sufficient resources.
That is why they can so freely assist others, particularly young teachers whom
Competitor-teachers would view as competition or even opposition.

Chad may have had a mentor, but he also seems to know that he would
work in a field that was based on relationships. Like most Mentor-teachers,
Chad was enticed into teaching because he could lead people to be the best
versions of themselves. Mentor-teachers have faith in the greatness of the
individual. They believe that some sort of success awaits each person.

Chad also values hard work, and that is how he was able to achieve his success. He is not married, and he does not have any children. He confesses that
his marital status is a dance with his profession. "I don't have a wife or kids
so I can throw myself into my work," he chuckles. "Wait, maybe that's why I
don't have a wife and kids!" When pressed, he admits that his long-term relationship with his girlfriend Sophia really should have resulted in a marriage
by now, "but she isn't about to drag me to the alter—not that girl. She has a
mind and life of her own. I don't think she is ready to share space with me."

After a few minutes of speaking with Sophia, one realizes that Chad's self-
deprecating comments are misplaced. Sophia would love to be married to
Chad, but not until he has settled down in his career and is ready to rearrange
his priorities.

Chad's rise to the principalship has been meteoric. He started and finished
his master's degree in administration during his first two years of teaching

high school mathematics. During the immediate next three years, he received a Ph.D. in education leadership.

Throughout his entire postsecondary education he built an electronic portfolio of his work. This impressive body of work, along with his reputation as a hardworking team player, made him very attractive to his superintendent. She also was familiar with this work because he volunteered for numerous district-wide committees, which he did as much to relate to his colleagues as to impress central office. In addition, he proved to be gifted at supporting union issues without angering or frustrating the administration. It really was not a surprise to any of the teachers at Chad's school when he was appointed to a principalship at a rival high school in the district.

Chad tells a different story about his quick rise to administration. "You know, a lot of people think it is because I am Black. They think I was put here because the district needed to show some diversity in administration." Chad looks away, but the hurt and anger are still evident in the lines that furrow his brow and cheeks. He goes on to explain that he is held to a different standard. "That's okay, though, because I can take it. I can reach any bar, but it still doesn't make it right. People ignore, or refuse to see, all of the hard work and time I have put into my professional career." At this point, one can imagine him thinking back to Mr. Williams and drawing on the support that an older, loving mentor can provide even through memory. The gift of believing in someone is a lifetime gift.

Because Chad is a Mentor-teacher, he may not even be clear himself as to who these "people" are. He bases his actions on love and respect, and when he believes he does not get the same in return, the anger blocks him from doing much helpful analysis of the situation. It is important to note that he "believes he does not get the same in return." Often the perception mentors have of others is flawed. They tend to judge the act of caring from their own perspective and use of the term. Obviously this is problematic—not everyone cares or shows caring in the same way.

In addition, Mentor-teachers become so accustomed to the praise they receive about how they nurture others and how "other-centered" they are, that they are, ironically, slow to realize when they are not. Indeed, Chad will tell you that his last girlfriend broke up with him because she claimed he was selfish. "She used to say that I did not take responsibility for my actions. I thought she was crazy and just looking for an excuse to end the relationship. But now, when I look back at my behaviors, well, maybe I just took the reputation of being 'other-centered' and got lazy about walking the talk."

Mentor-teachers are pretty good at self-reflection, especially after they let their emotions settle down. Just as Chad is able to look at how he may not be walking his talk, Mentor-teachers regularly evaluate whether they are making good on their promises, and though they might be slow at realizing hypocrisy, they get there. They understand deeply that keeping promises is a cornerstone of relationships built on care and trust. Since they hold this ideal so high, they are most frustrated by those who do not keep promises and commitments to them.

This probably is why it is so easy for Chad to blame Sophia for the lack of commitment progress in their relationship—he has had practice. While Chad's relationship with Sophia is not where he might want it to be, his relationships with his friends and his colleagues is something he is quick to brag about. "I have the best friends in the world—and many of them are right here in this school district." Catching his apparent hypocrisy, he adds "I know I said that lots of people think I have this position because I am Black, but it probably isn't really a lot of people—I don't know, I guess it just ticks me off. But, the friends I have, well they're the best."

Mentor-teachers are adept at making and keeping friends. In a nutshell, it is because they are kind and loving people who take their relationships seriously. And, even when they are irritating their friends with their over-zealous encouragement and prompting, the recipients of such attention are well aware that the Mentor-teacher is looking out for their best interests.

Students notice this as well. When following Chad down the hall of the school, one cannot help but notice the respect and smiles he is shown. "Yo, Doc," and "Hey, Doc Johnson," are heard over and over again. But Chad does not try to "fit in" the way some teachers do. "Kids, especially inner-city kids, can smell a hypocrite a mile away. They know who you are and who you aren't. Don't mess with that, or you lose them. I am a suit-wearing kind of guy, and I believe in hierarchy and respect. I am who I am."

Mentor-teachers want to make a difference in the world, and while they may want to prove to themselves and others that they have accomplished this, they really do not have much else to prove. They are comfortable with themselves. Like the environment that Chad has set for this school, the environment that Mentor-teachers establish is one that is authentic.

Being a Mentor-teacher is a rewarding and noble place to be. Chad could easily and happily continue to be a Mentor-teacher, and he could improve his capacity for unconditional love, or he could move on to the next Stage where he could develop alternate ways of knowing and increase his own understanding as well as service to children and his community.

ARE YOU A MENTOR-TEACHER?

Do you ever wonder if you should have been a missionary instead of a teacher? When there is a crisis or catastrophe somewhere in the world, do you want to pack up your things and go help? Do others comment on your compassion and empathy? Do people thank you for the attention and nurturing you have given them? If so, then there is little doubt that you are a Mentor-teacher.

Mentor-teachers are filled with compassion and the need to serve others, and they are most comfortable doing this in a defined and structured environment. They are described as good friends, and they have deep and enduring relationships. Although, it also is true that even with all of their compassion and empathy, they still can be control freaks. They like to know what is expected of them and what they can expect of others. They want this to be clear and consistent. This helps them know if they are successful at meeting their own goals, but more importantly, the expectations of others. They define the quality of their relationships in large part by their ability to meet high expectations and keep promises.

Many seasoned teachers will find that they are Mentor-teachers. It is a Stage that nicely balances the need to care for others with the ability to care for one's self and family. As we grow older, most of us become more understanding and more forgiving. These are cornerstones of the Mentor-teacher stage.

The Mentor is driven by the potential seen in everyone and is confident in his own abilities. As a Mentor-teacher, you truly are driven by love and your need to increase the amount of compassion in the world. You know you have power and you are confident in your ability to use it to help people or make a difference in something you care about.

You still are in touch with many of the attributes from both the Competitor-teacher and Protector-teacher Stages. Some may see you as over-confident and overbearing at times, but you are happy to use your influence on behalf of others and even happier to teach others how to best utilize their own powers and talents. You are a transmitter of love and seek to increase community service and altruism. While the Protector-teacher advocates for causes, the Mentor-teacher advocates for each individual.

Your Strengths

The Mentor-teacher is a mentor in the traditional sense of the word. He is a person who seeks to guide and inspire others. Sinetar (1998) presents five signs of a productive mentor that align well with the characteristics of the Mentor-teacher:

They affirm life and further its potential.
They enter into authentic dialogue because, at heart, they are genuine and
emotionally available.
They set clear boundaries for self and other.
They embody values and virtues others merely extol.

They stabilize people in a continuity of effort because they themselves are
   grounded.

As a Mentor-teacher, you are kind, attentive, and empathetic. As a result, you
have many friends and admiring colleagues. You have all of the loyalty and
nurturing of a Protector-teacher, but as a Mentor-teacher, you have become
skilled at tapping into empathy and employing individualized support.

   Whereas a Protector-teacher might believe that we should do unto others what we would have them do unto us; you, the Mentor-teacher, believe
we should do unto others what they would have us do unto them. There is a
definable shift of perspective from "I know what is best for you" to "show
me what is best for you."

   But, as a Mentor, you still are making the shift—it is what you are trying to
perfect. Mentoring is not leading others to their paths—although you might at
times shine light on a path. Rather, mentoring in this Stage is about showing
others how to find a path, get back on a path, or create a path, and it is done
judgment free. You understand that your path, or your idea of a path, is not
necessarily the right one for someone else. You take the time to find out what
someone needs from his or her perspective.

   You are able to do this because you seek to understand others, and you are
a good listener. You will remember the details of a conversation. You may not
remember what someone wore, but you will remember how they described
their feelings and how they presented their situation.

Your Challenges

Because Mentor-teachers are so comfortable in restrictive environments and
in controlling others, they run the danger of becoming counter-productive and
actually limiting their mentoring effects. As a matter of fact, while they are
motivated by love, this can at times be *conditional* love.

   Some potential mentees will see these aspects of the Mentor-teacher's personality first, and avoid the person in one-to-one relationships where Mentors really
shine. Other people will see the compassion and efficacy in the Mentor-teacher,
but soon grow fatigued at what they think is a personal agenda. You will be most
effective at making a difference in the lives of others if you can work on unconditional love and acceptance and letting go of your goals for other people.

Your Relationships

Mentor-teachers are motivated by the best of intentions. As a Mentor-teacher
you want to bring out the best in others. You might be driven by a need to get

people to behave a particular way; but it is because you believe it is the best for them. This is what you need to mediate—your need to mentor from your own perspective and paradigm.

Because you so easily see the beauty and potential in others, you can become relentless in your encouragement, indeed you probably are often excused of nagging. It is true, that for the most part, you are able to encourage and motivate others to higher levels of thought and action, but if you are not careful, your overzealous approach can cause some people to avoid you—especially those who are not in an emotional place in which they are ready to move and grow, much less hear about the mistakes they have made. Stay in your natural place of nonjudgment and go easy on pointing out the mistakes of others.

We likely have all been there—on the receiving side of a well-intentioned Mentor-teacher. They are good at keeping us honest with ourselves, so we avoid them when we are on a diet and ate six Oreo cookies, and we avoid them when we likewise are letting opportunities pass us by. Your job to be an effective Mentor is to make sure your approach is soft and balanced enough that you are not avoided too much.

As a Mentor-teacher, you may understand that part of your mission at this time in your life is to help others. If this also is part of your life path, then being a Mentor-teacher is going to be a wonderful stage for you: inspiring and invigorating. You know that you have figured out some things in life, and you want to impart this knowledge by modeling as well as instructing.

Fortunately, you would never intentionally manipulate another. Even when you are being overly controlling, you do not have a hidden agenda. It is in the Stage of Mentor-teacher that the teacher realizes that even if he came upon the Ring of Gyges (Book II, of Plato's Republic) he would not use the ring's power of invisibility in any way that would harm another or compromise his honor. He probably would not even use the power because it would, by definition, take choices away from others.

The Mentor-teacher is open to relationships with all kinds of people, but will move away from those who are unethical or manipulative. You may not always do this as quickly as you should because you tend to see the best in people and too easily discount the negative aspects of someone.

This openness and ease of forgiveness enables Mentor-teachers to reach out to many more people, but it also means that they can be hurt if they are not careful. Betrayal hits Mentor-teachers hard because it is something that they cannot understand and empathize with. They are shocked and saddened on a deep and personal level when lied to or manipulated, and they do not bounce back quickly. When you become a Creator-teacher, you will find that you still have a good heart, but you attract better things in your life and are more resilient as well.

You have come to understand the personal power you possess and you know where you have influence and how to use it. You see the goodness in others, as well as yourself, and you seek to create a sharing environment. You believe in the potential of individuals, but you see more potential when these individuals collaborate and unify their power and strength.

Therefore, as a mentor-teacher you enjoy collegial memberships, but you are quite selective in what you participate in. To you, all group activities are a way to learn more about others and a way to share more with others. Organizational membership then is a way to influence others and change what needs to be changed.

Your World

As a Mentor-teacher, you prefer an environment that is balanced. You like a balance between rigidity and flexibility; between rules and freedom; between teacher control and student control. You also seek harmony in physical surroundings as well as in personal interactions.

The Mentor-teacher understands that the world changes when individuals come together believing they can make a difference. He likes being a teacher because he believes he can change the world by motivating one student at a time to believe.

Your worldview is truly that—it is a view of people that transcends physical boundaries. You do not support government policies that treat people differently based on where they live. You might be patriotic, but you are not parochial.

As a Mentor-teacher, you generally feel the need to have a specific spiritual base, usually a dogmatic religion, but you are not judgmental of the views of others. As a matter of fact, even if it is contrary to your religious teachings, you will tend to believe that all people can find a path to heaven. Spinoza (1632–1677) told us that one must love humanity as well as God. This is something you as a Mentor-teacher innately understand.

You are skilled at combining faith and reason. As such, you might enjoy familiarizing yourself with the teachings of Thomas Aquinas (1225–1274) who believed that truth could be arrived at through both methods. This type of knowledge would be satisfying to your need to rely on your faith in your day-to-day activities while relying on reason for your curriculum development and instructional strategies.

You might also learn from St. Teresa of Avila (1515–1582) who was adept at combining prayer and action. She wrote of her mystical experiences in order to guide others, but she did not believe her mystical experience essential for others to experience. She believed in a God accessible to all.

Your Approach to Teaching

You, the Mentor-teacher, believe that the most important purpose of education is that it can teach people how to learn and how to love learning. Teacher and author Marva Collins noted: "I cannot build enough bridges for all of them, but I will teach them to have the fortitude to build their own bridges. To take paths never taken and always leave a path for those who may follow" (p. 244). This is your view as well.

Since your goal in education is not just to teach for understanding, but to facilitate lifelong learning, you will focus on instructional strategies that provide an opportunity for the student to seek deeper meaning and make connections to other aspects of his or her life. You encourage and even incorporate community service as a way to make learning relevant to your students and to teach them how we are interconnected and interdependent on one another.

Archived instruction is something that would suit you particularly well. You also would find enjoyment using hypothesis development and deductive inquiry—anything that would encourage your students to use critical thinking and wonder, such as getting them to predict, explain, summarize, and evaluate.

You also may want to incorporate KWL into your lessons. Prior to a lesson, ask your students what they know (K) and want to know (W), and then after the lesson, ask them what they learned (L). Not only can this improve your instruction as you find out what was learned compared to what you intended them to learn, it also gives the students some control over their own learning. Another way to give them control is to employ a method that is a great fit with the Mentor-teacher: micro-teaching. Have students take turns preparing and presenting lessons.

You typically do not have any problems with classroom management because students in your classroom are given a great deal of respect—this was carried over from your days as a Protector-teacher. But now, you also deal with problems by finding out what caused the problem and trying to be compassionate and preventative rather than punitive.

You operate from kindness and you expect your students to as well. Since you do, they generally do also. It is a peaceful environment that arises from this behavior, which you value. If you work in a school setting, you may even teach peace studies as part of your curriculum. If you are not doing so already, you should consider bringing into your classroom or school peer counseling and peer mediation.

As a Mentor-teacher, your curriculum development is best focused on student projects that are authentically measured. You understand that students have different learning styles, and as such, they have different preferences for demonstrating their skills and understanding.

As long as your students acquire the knowledge and skill, you do not care how they do it, and you do not care how they want to prove it to you. You allow presentations and the demonstration of learning in many forms.

An effective mentor uses spiritual intelligence (Sinetar, 1998). This means you rely on alternative ways of knowing. You do not just rely on what a student tells you. You watch her body language and her behaviors, and you listen to your intuition. If your intuition tells you something different from what a student is telling you, you respectfully probe a little deeper and try to reconcile the difference.

Because of your acceptance of alternative ways of knowing, you may believe that there are things and places that are sacred, and your lessons may reflect this. You may try to get your students to understand the concept of sacred and develop ways to more fully appreciate and care for things. You also may be interested in helping your students further explore how things are related to each other. Quantum physics would offer you interesting ways to bring this point across as well as having a green classroom.

Moving from Mentor to Creator:

Choice keeps you at this Stage. This is a successful and well-functioning Stage. A teacher can be happy at this Stage—and so can his students. The impetus for moving to higher Stages is your increasing desire to not just improve your teaching, but to improve your understanding of people and the meaning of life.

You understand that spiritually moving on from here has more to do with your personhood than your teaching. The positive characteristics of this Stage will follow through to each of the other Stages. In other words, once a Mentor, always a Mentor. This is because it is an act of compassion, and the Stages that come after this one all build on compassion.

Ironically, although it is true that being a good Mentor is an important aspect of spiritual development, one should not spend a great deal of time as a *mentee*. Ralph Waldo Emerson made the point in his 1838 address to the Harvard Divinity School graduating class: "Imitation cannot go above its model. The imitator dooms himself to hopeless mediocrity. The inventor did it, because it was natural to him, and so in him it has a charm. In the imitator, something else is natural, and he bereaves himself of his own beauty, to come short of another man's" (Emerson, p. 256).

In order to move to the next Stage, you need to keep your expectations of others high. Do not expect what you give. Expect more, but be patient. You need to nurture your faith in the ripple effect of mentoring and of good deeds. When you listen and guide, remember to let your mentees set their own bars rather than having you do it for them.

Also, learn that others show caring in different ways and realize that the act of caring is stepping into the place of another. Build on the empathetic aspects of your caring personality. If you want others to step into your shoes and understand you fully, realize that you need to open that door. You often can open it by simply stating your perspective and needs in a matter-of-fact way.

You need to trust in your own creativity and be ready to abandon your pride. Love what you do and create for its own sake. This means learning to care less about how others judge you and learning to move away from the need to be externally validated.

Lastly, you need to work on forgiveness. Forgiveness is the tool for change for Mentor-teachers. Forgiveness is something that humans have to actively work on in general, but if you want to move on to become a Creator-teacher, you need to exercise your forgiveness ability the way you would a muscle. Forgiveness improves you, as well as the object of your attention. Keep in mind what Nelson Mandela said "Resentment is like drinking poison and hoping it will kill our enemies."

You will know it is time to move to the next Stage, when you find yourself actively seeking out something more and see yourself more as a spiritual being who teaches than as a teacher who is interested in spirituality. When this is evident, it is time to make a conscious effort to adopt the characteristics of the next Creator-teacher.

It is at this point in the movement through the Stages—between Mentor and Creator—that one begins to realize, as did Spinoza, that God is all and all is God. Movement throughout the remaining Stages is more easily accomplished if you have the orientation of being fully connected to God at every step of the way.

Spinoza was a champion of free speech and religious tolerance, and you probably will find at this point, that you are becoming more open to the knowledge and voice of your students. The more you rely on this faith in others, the more readily you will advance to the Stage of being a Creator-teacher.

Keep in mind that your movement from Mentor to Creator will be something you do quite separately from other people. Most of your friends and colleagues, while they may be aware of your human faults and frailties, are not going to see you as someone in need of great improvement.

As you prepare to move to the next Stage, you may become conscious that you are giving up control to God, and because of your own search for spiritual awakening, you may become aware of the paradox of doing so. This paradox is described well by Paul Tillich when he describes prayer as speaking to somebody "to whom you cannot speak because he is not 'somebody,' of asking somebody of whom you cannot ask anything because he gives or gives not before you ask, of saying 'thou' to somebody who is nearer to the I than the I is to itself" (Tillich, p. 305).

Incorporating the Right Changes

As a Mentor-teacher you are adept at using authentic instruction and assessment, and you have developed ways to let students demonstrate their knowledge. As a Creator-teacher you will be more creative and bolder in your thinking. Use visuals whenever you are able. When you or your students are making decisions, use a decision tree to assist in the process.

Start now by letting your students do abstracting—summarizing and converting real world events into models. Letting students develop models is a way of giving them voice. Continue to look for opportunities that increase student voice. Help your students move from doing to expressing, from presenting to experiencing.

At this point in your career, you probably are conducting professional development or in some way guiding and assisting fellow teachers. If not, you should look into doing so. You would be good at it. But that does not mean that you should neglect your own growth, or have your growth solely be dedicated to how you can help fellow teachers. Keep in mind that you want to move to the Creator-teacher stage so find professional development opportunities that take you out of your comfort zone.

If you hate group work, make yourself do it. If you hate creating art projects, take an art class. When we get out of our comfort zone, we have to find new ways to present ourselves and new ways to cope. We have few tools at our disposal if we are in a situation that is new and uncomfortable, so we are forced to create something new. This act of creation not only gives us a new tool and perhaps a new method for tool building, but also we gain confidence in what we can do outside of what we know.

Incorporating Spiritual Practices

Below are Stage-specific practices designed to do two things: they will honor and celebrate the Stage you are at, and they will prepare you for the expectations of the next Stage. While it is your goal to develop into more advanced Stages, this will happen more quickly if you express understanding and gratitude for the Stage in which you currently are. Full appreciation for the wonderful person you already have become is necessary for spiritual growth.

Mentor-teacher Prayer

> *Thank you for today and for all of the love that surrounds me.*
> *Help those in the world who are sad and lonely,*
> *and who have suffered the loss of loved ones.*
> *Guide me as I seek to play a meaningful part*

in the lives of my students.
Help me to understand what they need
and to be someone who shows them the path to fulfill those needs.
Bless me with pure and supportive relationships
so that I have the strength to live the life I am meant to live.
Keep me always mindful of your love
and the power of love in the world.

Mentor-teacher Meditations

You will need to read through this entire meditation before you begin. It would be best if you could be outdoors where you can breathe deeply and fill your lungs with fresh air.

Sit in whatever position is comfortable. Spend a couple of minutes with your mind blank. See what thoughts come to you. To begin your Mentor-teacher meditation, close your eyes and picture a bright green light in your mind.

Picture yourself in flight. You can be yourself flying, or you can picture yourself as a bird. Feel the air on your face and your arms and hands cutting through it. Feel the power of soaring up and the freedom and release of gliding downward. Let yourself fly for a while. Where do you go? What do you see?

Contemplate where you went, why you went there, and what you saw. Write a message in the sky. What would you say? To whom would you say it? Now, go to the homes of people you love. Hover over each home and either thank them for the love they have given you or lessons they have taught you, or give them a wish or blessing—something that they want or would serve them well.

Mentor-teacher Journaling

Make a list of the things you love and admire about yourself. Make a long list.

Think of four people who love you. It would be best if these people represented different types of relationships, i.e., spouse, aunt, best friend, child. After each name, create two lists. The first list should be everything you admire and love about the person. The second list is everything you believe they admire and love about you. Compare these two lists to the first one you made about the things you love and admire about yourself.

What are the common elements? These are things that are important to you. Write affirmations using them. Your affirmations can look like these: "I am _____" "I give _____" "I am capable of _____" "I have _____"

Now, look at the list of what you love about others. Is there anything there that was not on the other two lists? If so, imagine yourself with those attributes as well, and write affirmations with them as if you already possess them.

Mentor-teacher Movements

Movements for Mentor-teachers should include touch. Giving or receiving massages would be particularly beneficial to the Mentor-teacher. If you have a partner to dance with, consider slow dancing with him or her. If such touch and movement are not possible together at this time in your life, you can still do slow dance movements alone. Tai Chi would be a wonderful way for you to move, strengthen your body, and express yourself.

Mentor-teacher Music

The Mentor-teacher should listen to keyboard music. Some suggested music is the following:

Adagios from any of the following masters: Beethoven, Rachmaninov, Mozart, and Chopin.
Scarlotti
Aquarium by Saint-Saens

The Mentor-teacher is summarized in the table below:

Table 4.1

View of self	Guiding
Motivation	To teach others how to improve their lives
Strengths	Generous; secure; trusting
Weaknesses	Unforgiving; controlling; zealous
View of others	As having great potential
View of God, spirituality	God is leading us. There is a divine plan, but we can get off track. God will always take us back. Religion is there to guide people on the right track and keep them there. Religious education and outreach is the very important.
View of education	Impart knowledge
Instructional strategies	Problem-solving
Classroom management	Through mutual agreement and contract
Use of curriculum	Expose to divergent ideas
Necessary to move a stage	Realize that trust can exist without knowledge

Stage 5

The Creator

When music changes, so does the dance.

—A Hausa proverb from West Africa

MAYA

Maya's quirky personality is effervescent and intense, and she exudes confidence. One expects to become inspired and creative just by being in her presence.

When we first met she referred to herself as "Maya, Maya, Maya." "That's what everyone calls me," and she demonstrates it by rolling her eyes, shaking her head, and singing her name three times in a row. "Do you think it means that people become exasperated with me?" she laughingly asks. Her eyes sparkle in that wise way that people with self-knowing have.

Because she likes herself, flaws and all, she becomes immediately likeable to others. These people—the ones who are so incredibly comfortable in their skin—are the most captivating of people. And, they usually are the Creators among us. This is the case because as Creators, they constantly are evaluating who they are, what they believe, how they act, and whether it still is relevant to the life they want to lead. This self-reflection, critical analysis, and course adjustments of Creators enables them to create themselves anew.

Their self-knowledge is strong, their views are fresh, and their confidence is assured. Their creative energy is palpable. It is hard to tell with some people whether being a Creator leads to change or if being open to change enables one to become a Creator. It appears to be a dynamic and invigorating cycle—one that is notably healthy and productive.

Maya is a Creator-teacher, and her comfort with herself is quite evident. Indeed, Creator-teachers are comfortable with everything. They are accepting of the world as it is presented to them. Because of this, they are able to focus on change that is positive—built upon new ideas, rather than that which is negative—built on the undoing of old ideas.

The focus on possibilities and potential is how Creator-teachers are able to inspire fellow teachers and students alike. Creator-teachers have a passion and ability to inspire the way Mentor-teachers have the passion and ability to guide. They challenge their students to approach most things in a new way.

Maya understands this about herself, and is proud. "I love that kids tell each other to take lessons from me. That's not an easy thing to have happen." She goes on to explain that she is glad that it happens, because she does not do any marketing or advertising. In looking at Maya, one might assume that she is teaching an elective art class. She sits across from me in a calf-length jean dress with a festively embroidered shawl in a multitude of colors. She looks a bit like an old hippy, but she is too young; she is in her late thirties.

Maya is a piano teacher who works out of her house. But, looking around her home I am sure that her students learn more than music. It is a fun and creative environment.

Maya's husband died a few years ago, before they had the chance to have kids. Many of her friends thought this tragedy would be the end to Maya's childlike enthusiasm for life. She and her husband were avid travelers and explorers. During the summer months, they would venture to foreign countries and immerse themselves in the culture, the food, and the art. These experiences, of course, inform Maya's teachings and how she presents the world of music. But when she returned from her trips, she rarely talked about what she saw and what she learned. She talked about what she felt, what she experienced, what she created—or what she planned to create.

Her house is not filled with souvenirs, but instead with creations she made based on what she saw. After her trip to Spain, she made a mosaic table; after her trip to Peru she made a drum; and after her trip to India, she made a sari. She takes this approach into her teaching. Her students learn music in a context. This is not just a habit with Maya, it is a philosophy.

She explains that a career is not a job path, it is a soul path. It is how you choose to express yourself. "By following your bliss," she tells me on more than one occasion, you choose your career. "And, you should make this choice regularly." Her point is that it does not matter how many or how few jobs or even careers you have in a lifetime, it only matters that at any given moment, it is what you choose to be doing. There was such power in her words.

After her husband's death, Maya took a year off from teaching. She was reclusive, rarely leaving the house or communicating with friends. No one expected Maya to go back to her old self. But she did. To hear her tell it, one day she woke up, planted flowers, painted her front door red, and began calling back her students.

Dealing with death is a severe example of how Creator-teachers go within, but it is an important example of how the creative process needs time for reflection and incubation—and the amount of time necessary varies depending on what else is happening in the life of the Creator-teacher.

Maya has many friends and many colleagues who enjoy spending time with her. This is because of Maya herself, but it also is true that Creator-teachers are hard to dislike because they truly are accepting and nonjudgmental of others, as well as spontaneously fun. Maya has friends of all ages. She has friends aging from their mid-twenties to their mid-seventies—close friends. She benefits from the various perspectives they have of life and history as well as the distinct differences among their family units. Maya has friends with young children and friends with young great-grandchildren.

In many ways, Maya's circle of friends looks like a village. One has to wonder if it is common for Creator-teachers to be involved with people of different ages and backgrounds. Certainly this would provide an abundance of inspiration and food for creative thought. What likely is true is that Creator-teachers seem ageless and draw people seeking to grow and create.

Most Creator-teachers are optimists—which is no surprise since they operate on faith and believe they can manifest their own realities. And, they can. The fact that they are optimists means that they tend to see the best in everyone. In fact, some of Maya's colleagues openly comment that she sees the best in people when she should not, and sees beauty where it is not. Maya knows this about herself. She understands that Creators such as herself are very trusting, and as a result, they are not particularly good with personal boundaries. It is not uncommon for them to turn off colleagues by oversharing or be taken advantage of by others.

To a Creator-teacher, everyone is a friend or a potential friend. No one is an enemy or a potential enemy. In the eyes of a Creator-teacher, it is okay to open yourself up to anyone and everyone because no one is going to misuse information or abuse power. At times this will prove to be naïve thinking and get the Creator-teacher in trouble or put her in harm's way.

Maya is well aware that others look at her as being too open and too self revealing. "People love listening to my stories, but afterwards, someone might say, 'You know, Maya, you really shouldn't have let them know thus and such, it gives too much of your power away.' I really don't know what they mean by that," she goes on to explain. "That really isn't how power works. It is not about knowledge. It is about truth, telling the truth, and always being a seeker of the truth."

We all have heard that knowledge is power. But, what Maya is trying to point out is that truth dissipates power. Truth makes benign the power that comes from knowledge because it just "is"—it is an end, it is not a means. More importantly, the main point that becomes clear with her words is that one does not really even need to be concerned with knowledge if one has faith.

Creator-teachers such as Maya will be quick to say that they have faith that they will be taken care of regardless of what misfortunes arise. Inconvenience, as well as outright heartache, gives energy to Creator-teachers. It does not mean that they enjoy life's hardships, but it does mean that they see them as part of life, and they use the pain for inspiration, energy, and regeneration. For them, there is not a wrong path—at worse, there is only a path that is temporarily uncomfortable. The ultimate force that they believe in is a protective and nurturing one.

Creator-teachers rely a great deal on faith. Much of their own inspiration and ideas are untested; that is what makes them creative. Because their actions often are untested, Creator-teachers have to trust that their intuition and judgment are worthy and workable. Maya is in a unique situation as someone who works rather isolated. In some ways, it is easier for her to be more creative, because her ideas are not as exposed to the critical eye of others until they are more complete. But, on the other hand, she does not have the energy and ideas of other people to incorporate into her teaching and creating.

Maya can continue to be a Creator-teacher and improve her discernment and enhance her communication skills, or she can develop both of them toward intuition and great wisdom by moving to the next Stage.

ARE YOU A CREATOR-TEACHER?

Do you find yourself continuously trying to improve yourself in demonstrable ways? Do you see play and discovery as preferred ways of learning? Do you value things for their beauty rather than their material value? Do you feel compelled to leave something of yourself behind? If so, you probably are a Creator-teacher.

Do not be concerned if you do not view yourself as "creative" or as an artist. This may just be a matter of semantics. We all are creative, and we are all artists; we just have to believe it and engage it more fully in all parts of our lives. The Creator does this, but she may not consider herself an artist or creator because her focus has been on the process rather than on the creation.

As a Creator-teacher, you seek to make yourself the best you can be. You constantly are looking for ways to make yourself a better human being—whether this is improving your intellect, your body, your relationships, your contribution to society, or your spiritual development.

However, this quest for excellence does not mean that you are overly serious. As a matter of fact, you take growth seriously, but you do not take *yourself* too seriously. You are quick to laugh, quick to make fun of yourself, and quick to use play and adventure as ways to learn and to teach.

You do value material objects, but you do so because of their beauty, not their financial worth. Your friends might buy their cars because of the value or even the bragging rights that come with certain makes; you on the other hand drive a car that you think looks fabulous, feels wonderful in your hands, or is the best vehicle to get you to a beautiful location. This is the same with your clothes. Creator-teachers are not beyond possessing beautiful clothes, but they do not collect designer outfits or seek to spend a fortune on their clothes because they can or because they want to say they did. Creator-teachers buy clothes that they think look beautiful, feel wonderful, and/or evoke certain feelings or memories.

These are not traits easily understood by others, and it is not easy to become a Creator-teacher in our rigid bureaucratic and materialistic society. Our culture does not celebrate the artist or her creations, much less uniqueness in everyday people. In addition, our culture is highly competitive with expectations that we will all value wealth as the ultimate goal and respect and participate in a hierarchy ensuring that only a few will reach the goal.

Another reason this Stage is difficult to advance into is because most of us are insecure about our creative and entrepreneurial sides. It is not something that generally is nurtured within our school systems or even within many of our families. Therefore, we are not confident that we are indeed creative or unique, and we certainly are not confident that others will appreciate what we create. Mentor-teachers might avoid becoming Creator-teachers based on fear of vulnerability. This fear of opening ourselves up as Creators as well as admitting this aspect of our connection to divinity can be very scary.

The Creator-teacher is motivated by self expression and guided by faith. If you are a Creator-teacher, you trust your own dreams and intuition and you are able to tap into a higher power to guide you in your life, including in how you instruct and communicate with your students. It also is manifested in how you guide them in their own creation process.

Indeed, you know by now that you are an adept communicator, both verbally and physically. You are able to get many points and ideas across with facial expressions and body language, but when you do use verbal expression it appears as an art form to others—pleasant to listen to and often captivating. Creator-teachers know how to turn-a-phrase, and this often is how you pull in your students and inspire them. Creator-teachers are motivated by a need to express.

It often is the case that Creator-teachers have exuberant personalities. This is because they are as free with themselves as they are with their thinking and their teaching. However, it would be a mistake to think that there are not quiet and introspective Creator-teachers. The Creator aspect of the teacher refers to her orientation to the world and her approach to teaching, not to how she presents herself to the world.

If you are quiet or introverted, do not think that this means you are not, or cannot be, a Creator-teacher. You will just express yourself a bit differently. You may find that you are willing to put yourself out there more and more as you spend time in this Stage.

You are connecting regularly to a higher power, and this gives you different knowledge as well as the confidence to share this knowledge with others. What you will ultimately experience as a Creator is the ecstasy that mystics have written about for centuries. As a Creator-teacher, you look for opportunities for your students to go within themselves to be guided by a deeper meaning as well, and then you give them opportunities to express the resulting creativity.

It would be no surprise to find a Creator-teacher working in the arts or the humanities, but since most of us choose our disciplines before we arrive this far in our spiritual development, we find that there are many different types of teachers at this Stage.

Your Strengths

The Creator-teacher has gotten to this point and generally thrives here because of her faith in self, others, and a higher power. That means that, as a Creator-teacher, you know to trust in your intuition and even your dreams. The Creator-teacher is a thriving person, and a teacher could stay at this Stage and be happy and content for the rest of her life. This is because this is the first of the Stages where a teacher combines the healthiest and most productive aspects of caring for self, caring for others, and listening to a higher power.

In addition to relying on their faith, Creator-teachers rely on integrity. As a Creator-teacher, you know that you are trying to do the right thing and be ethical at all times, so you trust your decisions and easily forgive yourself when you make a mistake.

If you are a Creator-teacher, you will find this integrity most evident in two ways: first, you prayerfully take things to God, and you listen—to your heart, to your intuition, and to any signs you get from God. You do not allow other humans to mediate these messages for you and tell you how you should think.

Second, you ask others how you are doing. You seek to find out from those around you where you fall short on your promise-keeping, veracity, caregiving, forgiveness, and gratitude. You take criticism to heart and you change your ways to make sure you are walking your talk. It is the assessment of your integrity that is most admired by others. They may be intrigued and impressed with products you create, but they mostly are drawn in by your ethics and your ability to fulfill your dreams. They know that, whether they agree with you or not, you are someone they can trust to be telling the truth and trying to do the right thing.

If you ask a Creator-teacher how often she prays or when and where she prays, she may respond by saying "I always am in prayer," or "I will turn to God at any given moment." You rely on a higher power with whom you communicate regularly. This could be in the form of many different types of practices. Perhaps you are involved in traditional religion, or perhaps something less traditional, but whatever you do, it involves regular communication with a higher being. Not only does this work for you in giving you a sense of peace and fulfillment, but also helps you in creating the life you desire.

Listening to that "still small voice" is the foundation of what makes Creators creative. Because their actions often are untested, the Creator-teacher has to trust that her intuition and her judgment produce worthy and workable creations. Some of this comes from time—time teaching and time moving up through the Stages—but much of it comes from a belief that there is something bigger and better out their guiding them . . . a higher force . . . a God who talks to them.

Theologian Matthew Fox ties it together this way: "Because of the unique inter-connection between creativity and compassion, between giving birth and giving birth to justice, there never was a true prophet who was not an artist nor a true artist who was not a prophet" (Fox, 1999, p. 133).

Your Challenges

Creator-teachers are constantly expressing themselves in various ways, but they need to watch their boundaries. This is for the comfort of others as well as their own protection. Whether you are an introvert or extrovert, you deeply enjoy the company of others. Make sure to trust your intuition though in deciding how open to be with others and how much to share. You can make a difference with people, and still be authentic, without giving away too much of yourself. Sometimes Creators forget that it is okay to have secrets and privacy.

As a Creator-teacher, you surely cut your own path. This artistic and experimental orientation of yours enables you to manifest results rather quickly and predictably. This is due to your connection with the divine, your personal creativity, and your growing detachment from unhealthy outcomes. Not everyone is ready to accept these abilities of a Creator-teacher, and you have to be careful not to appear either crazy or as a zealot. Be an example, and let people come to you with questions about how you are able to accomplish what you do and why you are as happy as you are.

The Creator-teacher can lose focus quickly. She tends to be a jack-of-all-trades, master-of-none. That is because she is intrigued and delighted by the potential to learn something new where she can immediately express herself. Today she is painting, but tomorrow she may very well be singing. This lack of focus is a disadvantage in many settings. Regardless of what grade or topic you are instructing, you are rarely seen as management material. That is too bad, because your creativity and risk-taking behavior is just what most educational organizations need to reengage their faculty, staffs, and children.

There are some dangers to putting a Creator-teacher in a position of power, however. Such teachers tend to be more focused on the journey then on the product. This is a wonderful attribute for gaining spiritual development and insight, but it is not sufficient in a management position where the budget and personnel reviews must get done. If you want to move up the hierarchy—and most Creators do *not*—you will need to work especially hard on developing a results orientation and recognizing the need for timelines.

Your Relationships

If you are a Creator-teacher, you might find that people can be intimidated by you. When this happens, you can usually tell, but you are still surprised since you see yourself as so open and receiving. Of course, once people get to know you, they like you, but you are not immediately approachable to everyone. Because Creator-teachers are comfortable with most everything about themselves, they are simultaneously confident, creative, and fun loving. Not everyone is comfortable among this personality combination. It is a very free personality—a personality that does not easily subscribe to cultural customs.

Creators are the people who push the envelopes, and indeed often create the new norms. The earlier spiritual Stages are made up of teachers who are more or less comfortable with the status quo, and the later two stages are made up of teachers who are not bound by the environment, so the people who are most able to envision and enact healthy changes to our environment and our systems are the Mentor- and Creator-teachers.

However, while the Mentor- and Creator-teachers are doing this, there are plenty of people who are frustrated by them and who believe they are on the wrong track. Those teachers who are particularly conservative may be captivated by the Creator-teacher, but they will not be comfortable with their seemingly careless attitude—an attitude that conservative stages, such as the competitor and protector might view as irresponsible.

As mentioned earlier, Creator-teachers also have to watch their boundaries very carefully. Because they trust others, as well as their own intuition, their knee jerk reaction to life is to throw caution to the wind. They tell more about themselves than they probably should, and they inquire more about others than is often necessary or polite. This can be particularly problematic when working with adolescents who are currently in the process of understanding and establishing boundaries. In addition, the Creator-teacher can become so enthusiastic about the journey her students are on, that the students can misinterpret this enthusiasm for special favors or attention.

The Creator-teacher is self aware, and does not take herself too seriously. However, as a Creator-teacher, you can be exacting in your expectations of yourself when it comes to spiritual growth. You read and study everything you can in the hopes of improving your life as well as the lives of others. You believe you can pass on knowledge and skills to others that will help them be more successful, especially in their spiritual development, but your primary loyalty is to yourself. When you were a Mentor-teacher you focused on your students, as a Creator-teacher, you now focus on yourself knowing that improvements made here will inevitably help your students.

The Creator-teacher does not look for anything in particular in others. You accept people as they come to you and you work to avoid judging them or their decisions. You have friends of all ages and outlooks, and you will see the best in them, as you usually do in yourself. As a Creator-teacher, you probably are comfortable with Kant's (1724–1804) categorical imperative. Kant told us that it was a moral law that we should never treat a person, including ourselves, as a means, but only as an ends.

Your World

The Creator-teacher can adapt to any kind of environment, but finds great success in those that do not restrict her. She is comfortable with a lot of stimuli, but she also understands the importance of meditation and sitting in silence. You have a practiced ability to retreat within yourself for contemplation and communion with God. Just as Thomas Merton (1915–1968) did, you understand the importance of contemplation and self-reflection as a path to truly communing with God. Merton viewed it as necessary to empty oneself and make space for God and his will.

As a Creator-teacher, you seek out balance in your environment because you understand the importance of both inward and outward thought, and inward and outward action. You also enjoy how new things appear and feel when there is the natural variety brought on by intentional change.

As a Creator-teacher you understand that rewards are infinite. You do not subscribe to scarcity theory or fear-based beliefs. You believe that all you need and desire is available for your taking, as it is for everyone willing to believe and apply this belief. But you understand that this is possible only when you are riding the crest and inviting into your life that which ultimately benefits your spiritual growth. Just as the lilies of the field do not toil, neither do you.

Formal religion likely has lost its importance to you. You need something more personal at this Stage. You still might enjoy the communal aspects of formal religion, but you probably will struggle with any forms of religion that try to define the undefinable by making God simple enough for humans to understand. You also will avoid religions that lead humans to judge each other, claim ideological superiority, or justify behavior you know to be wrong, under the guise of a greater good.

You no doubt believe that there are many paths to one God, which is contrary to the evolved dogma of some major religions. Instead, you have faith that you are personally and regularly guided by a higher force. Your own spirituality will be most supported and nurtured in traditions and rituals that are rich in acceptance and expression and not bounded by doctrine.

Certainly there are teachers in every stage who believe in a higher power and believe they are being guided by that force. How this influences the Creator-teacher, Leader-teacher, and Healer-teacher is quite different, however. The Creator-teacher does not just believe that there is a higher power and that this power is responsive to prayer, the Creator-teacher believes that the outcome of prayer is very much determined by faith. One would expect to hear a Creator-teacher say "believing is seeing," rather than "seeing is believing."

Creator-teachers do not need to have something proved to them. They believe that what they can imagine and what they desire will be brought to fruition through the belief in it. Instead of accepting an unhappy plight as "God's will" the Creator-teacher more likely will view an unhappy plight as a sign that their thinking and acting needs to better align with their true desires, and once this occurs, their prayers for improvement will be answered.

As one of my Creator friends often says "the universe will meet you half-way." Creator-teachers are adept at riding the Crest, and because of this, they are able to steer their course and they are able to manifest what they need and desire through intent, mediation, and faith.

Your Approach to Teaching

As a Creator-teacher, you see education as a way to equip students with tools such as critical thinking and self-reflection so that they might be truth seekers. You also see education as a way for students to learn about the world and other views so that they might see differences in perspective and understand their place in the larger scheme of things.

Instructional strategies where both you and your students can be creative are going to work best for you—especially if there is an opportunity for physical movement such as physically acting out a problem or a solution, or using music and dance to make a point or enhance a point.

As a Creator-teacher, your lessons should be filled with opportunity for student expression. This would include speeches and demonstrations, but also would include more creative expressions that arise from the students and allow for unique ideas as well as the presentation of those ideas. If you are a music teacher, encourage composition. If you are a dance teacher, encourage choreography. This is the type of instruction that benefits both you and your students.

In addition to experiential learning, which you likely have been using since you were a Mentor-teacher, you are going to want to regularly incorporate guided imagery and unguided open discussions and brainstorming. As often as possible, this should be focused around problem solving. But, make sure that you and the students are open to multiple paths to the right answer. Since you want your students to become naturally self-reflective, you should clearly point out this aspect of problem solving, and you should always have a debriefing session after large lessons in order to hear what your students have to say and see what more they can process.

As a Creator-teacher, you have a learning environment that looks and behaves differently than that of most of your colleagues, and you know this. Your environment is aesthetically pleasing and probably even fun, and it likely is filled with items created by you, your students, and people you care about. While this is natural for you, you also understand that such artifacts will further engage your students.

Engagement with students is extremely important to Creator-teachers, because you want your students to see quickly and easily how to enjoy learning and how to create opportunities on their life paths. You also understand that the teaching-learning relationship is symbiotic. Therefore, as a Creator-teacher, you create lessons that are lively and devoid of lectures, and your assessments are almost always performance-based.

Like the Mentor-teacher, you have what it takes to fully utilize authentic assessment, and in particular, project-based student presentations of learning and acquisition. As a Creator-teacher you will tend to be adept at utilizing your own professional experience as well as that of others. It will not be uncommon in your classroom for experts in many fields to make appearances and share their wisdom.

You are committed to continuous learning and development, and as such, your knowledge has a good chance of being current and research-based, which is a strong foundation upon which to gain confidence in your own best practices and their application in your classroom.

Because you are teaching from the heart and teaching for life, character development, instruction in ethics, community service, and encouragement of political activism are all things that will work well in your classroom. These are areas where you have developed strong competence, if not expertise.

Moving from Creator to Leader

As a Creator-teacher you are, for the most part, happy and confident that all is right in the world and as it should be. You are able to manifest much of what you want in life, and you find the beauty in that which you did not intend to manifest.

You find that your dreams come true and your wishes are granted. You are successfully riding the Crest, and coincidences no longer seem to be coincidences; you expect the unexpected and are amused when something happens just when it is needed. "Whatever you ask in prayer, you will receive, if you have faith" (Matthew 21:22).

When crises occur, whether in your own life or in that of others, you seek to solve problems, ease pain, and find ways to prevent a reoccurrence, but you do not assume that there is a punitive God, bad karma, or lessons to be learned. You just try to learn from every situation you encounter.

Kant (1724–1804) believed that time and space belong to our perception rather than to the physical world. In order to move to the Stage of Leader-healer, you will need to develop a personal understanding in what is real and what is illusion. This is another way to ask yourself what a miracle is and when and where it exists. Kant explained that the mind conforms to things, but things also conform to the mind. What does this mean for you? If cause and effect are merely constructs of our mind, what does that free you up to accomplish in your life and on behalf of humanity? What can you manifest?

The field of psychology has taught us that our brains seek patterns. Although our eyes will transmit much data to our brains, the brain can categorize and give meaning only to that which we have encountered before or believe is possible. Decartes (1596–1650) believed much the same thing. He told us to doubt everything because we can only perceive as true that which we perceive. He knew our perspective was limited.

In order to move forward spiritually, you need to believe in that which is traditional, unperceivable, and unbelievable—that which is impossible. You have to accept a field of infinite potential and possibility. You have to retrain and rewire your brain. It is highly recommended that you familiarize yourself with quantum physics, as this would give some scientific grounding to these spiritual theories—which you might find helpful.

It is time to move to become a Leader-teacher when you are ready to take on more spiritual responsibility—when you are ready to not just accept or even invite divine intervention in your life, but when you are ready to believe that you also are divine—that God created you in his image, that, as Jesus said, "the Kingdom of God is within you."

What keeps you at this Stage is the lack of understanding that there is still improvement that can be made to your life. There is spiritual growth that can be observed by you and those around you if you embrace it. You need to be less fearful of the sacrifices that are ahead.

You admire people whom you believe are more spiritually developed than you, but often times you think that, to become someone like this, you will have to give up some of your wild side—some of the fun, creativity, and abundance. This is not the case. Those things usually become less important, but they are not less attainable should you desire them.

In order to begin moving to the next Stage, the Creator-teacher needs to understand that the inspiration that comes to her as a creative force, can be harnessed to accomplish tasks with broader applicability to self and others. As a Creator-teacher you are adept at manifesting what you want, and you are aware of your powers to do so. What you have not figured out yet is how to control and target your manifesting, and how to lend its use to others.

You already have realized that you cannot change other people, but you can show them where the tools are so that they might change their own path and do their own manifesting. Since you are able to control what you bring into your own life, it is time to develop the skills to help others do the same. The first skill to develop, which is essential to move to the next Stage, is the ability to always remember that you are an inspirer of others and as such you must suspend your judgment of outcomes. Everything is as it should be.

Even as a Creator-teacher, you may not take the time for reflection and creation that you need. If this is the case, you will have difficulty moving forward through the Stages, and you are at risk of moving back to the Mentor-teacher stage, where creativity, and the contemplation that impels it, are not necessary. Be sure to take the time to reflect and mediate.

If you are on the Crest and following your intuition, you are in a safe place. But, it still behooves you to be cautious in whom you trust. It is from a place of vulnerability that you are able to create, but vulnerability opens you up to the manipulation, control, and psychological abuse (intended or not) of others. Creator-teachers should work on their boundaries if they want to move on to becoming Leader-teachers. Draw upon your optimism. You know that in every challenge—even in defeat and death—exists the opportunity for something new to be learned, understood, and created.

In other words, being creative takes a lot of energy. Because of this, the Creator-teacher also is in danger of developing habitual patterns just to ease the intensity. While this is the antithesis to creating, it is not hard for you to fall victim to habit. Creating patterns is a way of resting and regenerating creativity, but the inattentive Creator-teacher could find herself parlaying a pattern into a habit that just pretends to create.

Incorporating the Right Changes

As you seek to move to become a Leader-teacher, it is important for you to gain practice using instructional strategies that can elicit both wisdom and imagination. Having students write stories is one way to do this, especially if you let them fictionalize non-fictional—even scientific information.

You also should instruct your students on great thinkers and religions leaders from throughout history as well as from your discipline, and give them time to reflect on the lives and thoughts of these people.

As you seek to move to the Leader-teacher Stage, you will want to change your focus from issues of integrity and engagement to empathy and understanding. Have your students put themselves in the place of others whenever possible. Every situation has a multitude of perspectives. Show your students now to hold various perspectives. Ask them how their thinking would have been different had they lived at a different, specific, time.

Another topic to explore would be that of the collapse of societies (you may want to read Jared Diamond's books *Collapse* and *Guns, Germs, and Steel*). After your students have been exposed to societies that have collapsed, expose them to various religious and cultural views regarding the end of the world. Then ask them, when will the world end and why? It is this type of lesson that will engage both you and your students at a deeper level of thought and spiritual exploration.

Professional development at this point in your spiritual quest should include specific content areas that you need to learn more about in order to be wiser. This would include more information about other religions, myths, cultures, and political beliefs—not just things in your own field. If you do not already possess a lot of knowledge regarding constructivist theory, it would be important to acquire that now. And, try to ascertain how your views were constructed and how you continue to construct them.

Incorporating Spiritual Practices

Below are Stage-specific practices designed to do two things: they will honor and celebrate the Stage you are at, and they will prepare you for the expectations of the next Stage. While it is your goal to develop into more advanced stages, this will happen more quickly if you express understanding and gratitude for the Stage in which you currently are. Full appreciation for the wonderful person you already have become is necessary for spiritual growth.

Creator-teacher Prayer

Thank you for all of the beauty and wonder
you have created in the world.
Help those who are struggling to appreciate the wonders around them
and let them be inspired to create a new path for themselves.
Guide me in my daily interactions with my students
that I might help them express themselves more fully.
I know that it is through such expression that I can
better understand and teach them.
Bless me with the ability to recognize and always
speak the truth,
and keep me aware of what it means to be
a person of integrity.

Creator-teacher Meditations

You will need to read through this entire meditation before you begin. Sit as comfortably as you can. Spend a couple of minutes with your mind blank. See what thoughts come to you. To begin your Creator-teacher meditation, close your eyes and picture a bright blue light in your mind.

Picture yourself walking through a large city toward a central park. Walk into this park, to the center of it. In that park is a covered gazebo. It is empty. Sit down in it. Relax.

Now invite a deceased loved one to join you. Sit across from this person. Hold hands. Tell this person what you would like him or her to know. When you are done, hug him or her, and invite in another deceased loved one. Do this until there is no deceased loved one that you feel you need to talk to.

Now, invite in the spirit of a living loved one whom you owe an apology. Have him or her sit across from you. Again, hold hands. Tell him or her what you are sorry for and why you are sorry. Hug him or her and send him or her on his or her way. Do this for everyone to whom you owe an apology.

Next, invite in the spirits of a living loved one you want to thank. Repeat for others you want to thank. Next, communicate with those from whom you desire something. Express your desire, hug them, and send them on their way.

Creator-teacher Journaling

Write a list of things that you have wished for that have come true.

Next, write a list of coincidences that you have observed. Write briefly about how you think these coincidences are related to wishes coming true.

Now, write a list of your current wishes. Write these as intentions rather than as wishes. In other words, do not say "I hope to . . ."; instead say "It is true that . . ."

Creator-teacher Movements

As a Creator-teacher it is important to explore roles with your movement. You can do your own interpretive dance to music, act out a theatrical role, or do an ethnic dance in costume or with elements of a costume.

Creator-teacher Music

The Creator-teacher should listen to singing or chanting. Some suggested music is the following:

Lama Gyurme and Jean-Philippe Rykiel: Lama's Chants
Benedictine Monks of Santo Domingo de Silos
Gregorian Chants
Joanne Shenandoah
Mari Boine

The Creator-teacher is summarized in the table below:

Table 5.1

View of self	Manifesting
Motivation	To create harmony
Strengths	Intuitive; balanced
Weaknesses	Too experimental; lack of good personal boundaries
View of others	As having the ability to create and manifest
View of God, spirituality	All God's people are good. Give people the facts, and they will make the right decision. Religion needs to change to be relevant. Miracles are not things of the past. Peace is most important.
View of education	Create knowledge; create equality
Instructional strategies	Applied learning
Classroom management	Out of respect for teacher
Use of curriculum	Enhance student voice
Necessary to move a stage	Understand how and why manifesting works and its relationship to knowledge

Stage 6

The Leader

Have you a gift which God has placed in your hands on which to play heavenly melodies which draw our hearts toward the beautiful in life?

—Kahlil Gibran

AMIRAH

Amirah seems saintly—simultaneously touchable and untouchable. She seems familiar and huggable, yet at the same time, she seems distant and remote, as if she is somewhere else.

Both of these aspects are apparent in her eyes. They are probing, and they give the appearance that she knows you, understands you, and likes you. This also gives the impression that she has some sort of understanding that allows her special perception and powers. You feel pulled away from yourself as you look into her eyes—as if you are traveling to a more comfortable space.

She does not seem controlling or even intimidating, it is more that she has a self-confidence that permeates the air around her and travels from her gaze right to your inner-being, and you greet her there. She is quick to smile, which provides relief from the feeling of vulnerability that she so quickly evokes.

I believe Amirah to be in her late forties or early fifties. She is dressed professionally, yet comfortably in something you might picture on the cover of a JCPenney's catalog. She walks through her classroom giving individual attention to her charges as she walks between the desks. She seems oblivious to all of the side conversations going on as if she has spent years as a bus driver or preschool teacher.

It appears that Amirah has more special education students than what would be expected in one classroom, even in this working-class industrial town where the special education rate is growing. When asked about it she seems pleased with the situation: "Oh, yeah . . . well . . . I encourage Principal Connie to give me these kids. Some teachers just aren't good with them."

So, how does Amirah know that she is good with them? And more importantly, how is it that she has the energy to take on what so many of us fear? When I ask her those questions, she becomes defensive at first. "It isn't about me—that's not why I do it."

This reaction is not uncommon from Leader-teachers. They often take on challenges as well as put themselves in positions of notoriety. It is not uncommon for others to take this as a sign of the Leader-teacher needing to gratify personal needs or receive validation from others. This is not the case, and it makes Leader-teachers jumpy. They generally are focused on others, and become frustrated—even hurt, when anyone views and judges them through a different paradigm.

As strong as they are, Leader-teachers are only human, and they exist in the same culture as the rest of us. That means that even they can feel insulted and slighted. That is often missed by people around them who tend only to see their strengths and leadership qualities. In addition, Leader-teachers know that they are role models, and they do not want the true nature of the role to be missed. To them, their true role is one of altruism.

Amirah catches herself, and before I have time to rephrase my question in a more tactful way, she continues: "I know what the challenges are like. I have a son who is autistic—Asperger's—and a daughter who was in a wheelchair for almost a year . . . and I was in speech therapy for three years when I was a kid. I am comfortable around human diversity." She stops abruptly, almost as if she wants me to digest what she just said. And I do. I indeed am struck with her description of special education as "human diversity."

As for her own children, Amirah has four, in two groups of two. She has two daughters from a previous marriage, both in college, and she has a stepson and stepdaughter, ages seven and nine.

Amirah became so interested in college life when she began exploring options for her daughters that she decided to do adjunct teaching at the local community college. This is where she met her second husband, a young community college instructor in mechanical engineering. He had custody of his two children, and to his surprise and delight, this was a bonus in the eyes of the child-loving Amirah.

When the younger kids are a bit older, Amirah plans to complete a Ph.D. in counseling to round off her experiences and open more doors, but for now she is delighted with the busy life her new marriage has afforded her. When asked why someone who is so obviously content would seek a new profession, she is quick to tell me "change is what life is about." She adds, "If I am not changing, I am not living, and if I am not living, I am taking up space on the planet."

I appreciate her perspective on change and how important it is for human spiritual growth, but I had to inquire further about her planned change. "Won't you miss teaching elementary school?" I asked. I barely finish my question before she explained to me that her career and the age of those she serves are irrelevant: "No, we all need the exact same things, no matter how old we are." Leader-teachers are wise, I thought.

I ask Amirah if she will miss her colleagues when she changes jobs. "Oh, no . . . I will stay in touch with them." She seems convinced, but I am not. Leader-teachers are an independent bunch, and while they have close friends, it is the friends who usually have to take the initiative. Leader-teachers value their relationships, but not as much as they value their independence, freedom, and solitude.

Leader-teachers have a deep understanding of people—at both the universal level and the individual level, and because of their strong intuition, they know their place in various relationships. This means they do not need reassurance in their relationships, and they do not need frequent contact or close proximity.

Their relationships flourish across time and distance. They know what their missions are on this planet, and they know that each of us has our own. That often means not staying in one place for long. Leader-teachers also know that they have special gifts that can get entangled or misdirected by human emotion, and they guard against that—usually by seeking time alone.

Amirah tells me this of the human condition: "We may need to join up with others to accomplish important tasks, but at our essence, we are each alone. We are born alone; we die alone; we make our spiritual discoveries alone; and we grieve alone. Our important journeys are all internal. I will stay in touch, but I really do not know what that means. I cannot now predict what that looks like in time and space. But love survives."

I admire her, but I wonder how many would not . . . do not admire this seeming disconnect from others. Her outlook seems Zen, but also emotionally distant. She seems wise, whole, and happy, but I cannot help but wonder if she is lonesome. Then I see the pictures of her husband and friends on her desk, and I think to myself "alone, often; lonely, never."

It is not that Amirah does not emotionally engage with others, it is just that she does not get caught-up in the drama. Leader-teachers rarely feel sorry for themselves or become pessimistic, which makes them adept at comforting friends and relatives. They are able to stick to facts and avoid overlaying any of their own biases or baggage. They stay emotionally detached, yet emotionally supportive. They are spiritually attuned enough to know what people are struggling with and are able to provide either nurturing, diversion, or a nudge, whichever is necessary. They understand that human dramas can be painful, and they can be empathetic without entering the drama. Their intention is to guide others out of their dramas.

In her interactions with her students, Amirah demonstrates how well Leader-teachers are able to provide wise counsel, even to young people. Typical of a Leader-teacher, Amirah is good at lending a listening ear and responding to where the other is.

Amirah's colleagues appear to fall into two distinct categories: the majority, who adore her, and a few, who like her, but are a little suspicious of her. This may seem to be a surprising finding at a final stage in spiritual development, but Leader-teachers can rub people the wrong way, because their lives often provide a mirror to others—and many people do not like what they see in their spiritual reflection.

Leader-teachers, with and without trying, demonstrate through their words and actions how an intuitive, peaceful, and magical life can be lived. When colleagues see that a great life can be manifested, and then see that they themselves fall short of accomplishing it, the Leader-teacher may become a source of frustration, object of envy, and a reminder of failure.

To make matters worse, Leader-teachers are truth speakers. They will point out what is wrong, unjust, and hypocritical. None of us likes to feel that we have fallen short, made a mistake, disappointed others, or behaved unethically. It takes time for people new to Amirah to understand her style, and Amirah in turn probably needs to work on projecting the compassion in her heart rather than the judgment others might fear.

Amirah must be careful, however, that she does not over-intellectualize her experiences. Leader-teachers love knowledge, philosophizing, and teaching. If they are not careful, they can literally over-describe and over-explain to the point that they mask the simple beauty of how potential realities await command.

Amirah contemplates aloud whether she does the opposite in her relationships. "I think I over-intuit my relationships. I think I should give more thought to others and how I interact with them. Sometimes I get the feeling that I am trusting my intuition instead of seeking knowledge."

She is right to have this concern. What she means here is that she has the tendency to assume what people need or want from her and their relationships with her. Because her intuition is so strong and people are so comfortable around her, she often doesn't ask people what they need or want. It makes me think of the person who misplaces the television remote, and in frustration decides not to watch television, instead of realizing that he could just get up, walk over to the television, and turn it on.

Also, by not giving others the opportunity to present their perception of a relationship as fully as possible, the Leader-teacher maintains too much control, and this can undermine unconditional love—which really is not unconditional—it is conditional upon truth, including understanding the other person's truth.

Amirah can continue to be a Leader-teacher and work on accepting wisdom without seeking to control it, or she can move to the next Stage where this will naturally happen as she more fully connects with the unknowing knower and does not need to put language and rules around her own understanding.

ARE YOU A LEADER-TEACHER?

Do people act as if they know you, when in fact they really do not—they just feel comfortable around you? Do you feel that you have a particular and important mission on earth? Do others tell you that you have guided them or inspired them in some way? Do you find yourself deeply committed to the ones you love, yet detached from their basic needs—almost as if you know things will work out and that the lessons before them, even painful ones, are lessons they need to learn? If this all seems familiar to you, you are a Leader-teacher.

There are not as many Leader-teachers as you might assume. The term leader here does not refer to roles that people may take on, so do not make the mistake of thinking that managers or school administrators are in fact Leader-teachers. They generally are not. A Leader-teacher is a spiritual leader and is generally quite aware of it. Teachers at any Stage may find themselves in positions of leadership, but a Leader-teacher transcends the role of managing.

As a matter of fact, Leader-teachers are not particularly comfortable with hierarchical systems. As a Leader-teacher, you will not be comfortable holding yourself out in a role that you or others may perceive as superior to others. While you understand that you have some talents and gifts that can guide and facilitate others on their spiritual paths, you do not see yourself as better than or greater than any other.

As a Leader-teacher, you primarily are a seeker of truth. You have found your place on earth, and you are adept now at using different ways of knowing to develop deeper understanding and compassion. Your leadership of others is driven by this compassion as well as divine inspiration. You are now transformational, and you prepare those who follow you to become leaders in their own right. At this point in your spiritual development, you are finding that Mentor-teachers and Creator-teachers especially are drawn to you.

A Leader-teacher wants to continuously learn. She is captivated by knowledge and how it can be used to evolve human thinking and solve human problems.

She desires to advance human spiritual growth. If you are at this Stage, you have learned that there are multiple ways of receiving knowledge, and now you seek to pass this information on to your students, colleagues, and friends.

At this Stage, you are more than intuitive, you tap into the divine. You operate so fully on the Crest that you are able to bring into your reality that which you desire, and when you do not get what you want, or you get something you do not want, it does not take long for you to see that either you have not been honest with yourself, or there is an innate conflict between your higher self and your human longings.

When you are in this Stage, you present to the world a strong sense of self and a connection to your place on earth. You are noticed, not because of your physical characteristics, but because you control your energy and command respect and guidance. You can just enter a room or a situation and the energy will change. Even if you were oblivious to your impact on others—and you probably are not—people tell you this all of the time. You are described as charismatic even if you are quiet. Even if you do not intend to take on a leadership role at work, you will find that you have followers there as well as in your personal life.

People are drawn to your confidence, sense of purpose, outlook on life, and imagination. You are able to blend intelligence, emotions, and spirituality together, and this resonates with people. Whether they know why or not, people are comfortable around someone who is authentic in that they do not expect themselves or others to divide the self. People who know you value your wisdom, but they also value your delivery. People feel better when they are around you.

Your Strengths

Leader-teachers are kind, generous, and easygoing. They appear to be rather Zen like—that is they take life as it comes without getting very ruffled. As a Leader-teacher, you expect that there will be sadness along with happiness and struggle along with peace, but you believe that the one thing of which you always are in control is your own reaction to what happens to you.

You choose how to react, and you continuously aim for a reaction that is calm and tempered because you know it is better for the mind and body and more likely to be a foundation for accomplishing something. Of course, by the time you are a Leader-teacher, this does not take much effort. Not much bothers you because you are not judgmental of others, you control your own life, and you attract goodness.

As a Leader-teacher, you are wise. Aristotle said that wisdom is the ability to at once see the universals and the particulars. It is the ability to blend various ways of knowing with the ability to appreciate applications and ramifications. "[Wisdom] is not contextual understanding that sits idle; it is the ability to apply and to appreciate the application of understanding. At its most fundamental level, it is the use of knowledge in light of spiritual purpose . . ." (Jax, 2005).

As a Leader-teacher, you employ whatever is necessary in order to discern what has brought about a particular circumstance and what is likely to bring about the outcome that delivers a higher purpose. It is your quest for true wisdom that enables your contentment and true leadership of others.

Wiggins and McTighe (1998) in their description of the six facets of understanding, describe someone as wise who is "deeply aware of the boundaries of one's own and others' understanding; able to recognize his prejudices and projections; has integrity—able and willing to act on what one understands" (p. 77). A Leader-teacher, then, is one who is continuously learning, seeks to apply that learning, reflects on her own worldview, acts ethically, and seeks out opportunities to learn—including through mystical experiences.

The one thing that the Leader-teacher generally struggles with is her frustration when she is seemingly unable to teach others how to ride the Crest and do their own manifesting. As a Leader-teacher, she feels no competition with others because she sees abundance in everything. Instead she seeks to bring out all potential in those she encounters. She wishes she were better at helping others achieve their highest spiritual development.

No doubt, many Leader-teachers have underestimated what they have taught others. However, Leader-teachers cannot help but be examples to others even when they are not consciously teaching or modeling. The gifts of Leader-teachers, particularly the ability to manifest, do not go unnoticed by those who spend time with them. Those who are open to spiritual development will pay particular attention to how Leader-teachers think and behave, and they will pick up on some of the necessary attributes, namely, clear intentions, deliberate actions, faith, and patience.

It does not take long for the spiritually eager to see that the Leader-teacher rides a Crest, and they eventually will seek guidance as to how to do the same. They soon realize that the universe will answer them when they state a desire and believe it will come true. The Leader-teacher needs only to share her truth.

If you are a Leader-teacher you understand that you have the ability and obligation to inspire others toward the divine. While you may never have had any concept of spiritual Stages, it is likely that you have known on some level most of your life that you would eventually be a leader of others—and since you always have had some identifiable connection to the divine, you probably suspected that you would or could be a spiritual leader.

Your Challenges

As a Leader-teacher you know your place on earth and how to use your senses and gifts to control your environment. This gives you a lot of confidence. This also is heady stuff, and if you are not careful, you can lose potential followers who are turned off by what appears to be arrogance.

Another danger that a Leader-teacher faces is the willingness, even eagerness, of others to turn themselves over to her guidance. Because it is readily apparent that you, as a Leader-teacher, are able to manifest your desire and walk easily through turmoil and conflict, other people are happy to turn their own power over to you as well. This can be enticing to you—especially if you are a new Leader-teacher who wants nothing more than to help.

However, making decisions for others is not the same as leading them. This may be harder for you to apply if you have a high IQ and therefore arrive at solutions more quickly than others. It is too easy to take on the responsibilities that belong to another and actually become part of the other's life lessons.

Your Relationships

The Leader-teacher has many friends, but spends much time alone. While it is true that you need your friends for emotional support and nurturing from time to time—especially those who are similarly situated spiritually—for the most part you are the caregiver in your relationships.

Leader-teachers are only human though, so this can at times lead to melancholy. Humans need the attention, care, and appreciation of other humans. Sometimes, however, as you become more connected to a higher power and divine messages, you tend to neglect your human needs—especially your needs for community and to be the recipient of nurturing.

As a Leader-teacher, you have many types of people in your life, but your own friends are spiritually in tune with you. You either recognize that you have something to accomplish together on the planet, or you are operating at the same spiritual Stage so you are able to counsel and support each other in ways that others are not.

As for your collegial relationships, you may not see a personal need for collegial organizations, but groups may develop around *your* beliefs or works. Your leadership is transformational, so you should allow this to happen. You do have a message, and you should not be fearful or humble. Embrace what you have to give even to increasingly larger audiences.

Your World

You are highly adaptable and can live and work anywhere. You prefer to be in settings that are filled with nature and beauty, but you are more concerned with being in an environment where your spiritual gifts are used—so geography is relatively unimportant to you. You go where you believe you are called, so you are open to geographical moves.

The Leader-teacher sees the world from a spiritual, emotional, and rational perspective. You are able to effectively blend all of these together. While you are operating from a more spiritual level and able to manifest what it is you need and desire, you still spend time in your head. You appreciate the abilities of the brain and the mind, and you use quiet reflective time to not just listen to the still small voice within, but to actively think as well.

You understand that spiritual growth is dependent upon the soul's connection to a higher power as well as its connection to your mind's interpretation of the facts of the world. You probably would appreciate the words of Albert Schweitzer:

> "[t]he spirit of the age rejoices, instead of lamenting, that thinking seems to be unequal to its task, and give it no credit for what, in spite of imperfections, it has already accomplished. It refuses to admit, what is nevertheless the fact, that all spiritual progress up to today has come about through the achievement of thought, or to reflect that thinking may still be able in the future to accomplish what it has not succeeded in accomplishing as yet." (p. 171)

The Leader-teacher is tolerant of the choices made by others, but has become more exacting about her own choices. Like Kierkegaard (1813–1855), you understand that true faith means having a lifestyle that is consistent with those beliefs. But, you also understand that this is a matter of faith more than of reason. Kierkegaard put it this way: "If I wish to preserve myself in faith I must constantly be intent upon holding fast the objective uncertainty . . ."

Faith for you is not a resting place or a justification when trying to figure out and reconcile dogma, doctrine, or the wishes of others. It is what sustains you as you seek to strengthen your spiritual understanding and live a life that is consistent with those beliefs.

You are a seeker of truth, but this need goes beyond a reach for heaven. One of the things you hope to do as a Leader-teacher is help your students also become seekers of truth. You know that this is not easy. You know that it is difficult and uncomfortable to try to untangle truth and reality from the human constructs to which we give the same names. Just remember that the idea of common truths does not mean homogeneity.

As a Leader-teacher, you appreciate the cultural diversity of the planet, and you see cultural competency as a necessity for spiritual growth. One of your primary goals is to find universal truths and common realities on which to build so that others have a jumping-off point for the exploration of their personal truths and personal realities.

The Leader-teacher's search for truth leads into the realm of mysticism for it is in the letting go to the divine that we ultimately find the truth. Author Ursula King (2001) describes a mystical experience as something that lies "at the very depth of human spiritual consciousness. It is one of great intensity, power and energy matched by nothing else" (p. 5).

Once you become a Leader-teacher, you probably are aware of mysticism and have no doubt had your own mystical experiences. At this point in your spiritual development you are seeking out such personal relationships with the divine. It probably is through such mystical experience that you have come to understand that we are all one—sharing the same molecular energy. However, you are an avid reader and thinker, so you may have come by this knowledge through exposure to quantum physics. Renowned quantum physicist, Dr. John Hagelin, the leading world authority on unified quantum field theories, is adamant as a scientist that the fundamental truth of unity is that we are all one.

Your Approach to Teaching

According to theologian and author Matthew Fox (1995), the Celtic people only allowed poets to teach because they understood that knowledge that does not pass through the heart first is dangerous. You also understand this. As a Leader-teacher, you are not afraid to show compassion for your students and for them to see your compassion for all living beings.

Like Christian mystic Teilhard de Chardin (1881–1955) the Leader-teacher also understands the importance of spiritual action that can bring about transformation. Teilhard de Chardin believed that what humanity needs most is to harness the power of love. The Leader-teacher also understands the power that resides within the energy of love and its potential to transform individuals and the world.

Leader-teachers use the energy of love in all that they do. This means that they try to improve more than just themselves and their students. They try to make life better for as many people as they can. So, as a Leader-teacher, you probably are most comfortable doing action projects and action research in your classroom, or any similar project where you can help produce a product or behavior that changes systems and situations in order to improve lives. Dialectic journaling is a great way for your students to capture their experiences and their thoughts about them.

You understand that coming from a place of love means being truthful as well as compassionate. Therefore, you are quick to admit when you do not know something and to admit to yourself and your students that there is plenty that you can learn from them. Carol Ann Kenerson (2000) in an essay in *Schools that Learn*, points out that "not having the answers is one of the greatest ways to arrive at a true solution" (p.115). You give students the freedom to explore including those areas where you do not have any expertise.

One instructional strategy that helps get students exploring answers for themselves is assumption smashing. Regardless of the topic, have students make lists of assumptions, and then have them work together to disprove them. Another strategy that is helpful in this endeavor is consequential exploration, where the questions you pose to your students are framed as "if this, then what?" This can be done at most any age.

To make this activity even more relevant to your students, have them look at aspects of their lives and see where such consequential exploration leads them. Enhance their ability to think critically and to analyze by helping them integrate new knowledge with known experiences to see what kind of alternatives they can imagine.

As you work to help your students think for themselves, make sure to include techniques you developed as a Creator-teacher so that your students are using their creativity as much as possible.

Ideally at this Stage, you would want to instruct and support your students in using alternative ways of knowing. However, if you are a public school teacher, it will not really be plausible for you to integrate blatant spiritual activities such as meditation, ritual, and prayer, and it may even be difficult to incorporate paranormal exercises such as remote viewing. However, you can instruct your students on what other cultures have experienced and believed. If they are in a mode of creativity, they will be able to apply this information in a more individualized and personal manner. You also can incorporate quantum physics in order to help them investigate the increasingly thinning line between science and religion.

As a Leader-teacher, your classroom is lively and interactive and there seldom is conflict or a discipline problem. This is because you treat your students with respect, and they in turn offer you respect and honor your position of guidance. It is clear to most, if not all of your students, that you are in a collaborative relationship with them in order to create knowledge, build wisdom, and enhance their lives.

The creation of knowledge and the building of wisdom are important to you. Therefore, your students are introduced to world religion, philosophy, and their historical context and when you create curriculum, you utilize all of the tools in front of you, most noticeably competencies based upon action research, reflection, and critical thinking. You measure your success in the increase of student knowledge and mastery of competency, and you do so through student projects and portfolios.

Moving from Leader to Healer

At this point in your life, you are successful at pretty much all that you do, because you rarely get off of your path or off of the Crest. You are living the words of Jesus: "Ask, and it shall be given you; seek, and ye shall find; knock, and it shall be opened unto you. For everyone that asketh, receiveth; and he that seeketh, findeth; and to him that knocketh it shall be opened" (Matthew 7:7–8). You are manifesting what you need and you are communing with God regularly, so you are clear and accurate about what you need and what would serve a higher purpose for you.

Moving from Leader-teacher to Healer-teacher involves conquering the fear of giving yourself up completely to God. As a Leader-teacher, this may be fearful to you. You may think that you have to give up your thinking and dedication to reason. That is not the case. Philosopher Ken Wilbur (2001) demonstrated that mysticism is not sacrificed by the use of the intellect when he explained how great physicists-turned-mystics relied on "sustained use—not of emotion, not of intuition, not of faith—but a sustained use of the critical intellect" that compelled them to look beyond physics altogether (p. xii).

Still, do not over-intellectualize. This is the time to get out of your head and rely more on your feelings, intuition, and revelations. Have faith that God communicates with everyone, and it is your choice to listen and your destiny to hear. While we can benefit from the wisdom and insight of others, no one needs an intermediary to communicate with God. Do not allow yourself the arrogance of believing that arriving at an advanced Stage makes you better or closer to God. You are a guide to God's path, not the path.

You will have a sense when you are moving on to the next Stage. You will feel your connection with God deepening and any metaphysical experiences will seem more to be in response to your goals rather than something random that happens to you. As you move to the next Stage, you will become more connected to the collective unconscious, group needs, and the needs of the planet. Your family and friends will sense this detachment from the more superficial needs that have brought all of you great fun and diversion. You may feel their conflict as they unknowingly *seem* unsupportive of your spiritual goals and changing habits. Remember the importance of community and fun. You can enjoy the superficial, without embracing it.

For moving forward, it is helpful to once again revisit the thoughts of Kierkegaard who believed that we must act in order to experience our existence. A passive life will not allow us to fully exist. He understood the fear involved in continuing to evolve spiritually. He also saw spiritual development in stages, and he believed the final stage involved courage: "it is terrible to jump into the open arms of the living god."

Incorporating the Right Changes

If you are not doing so already, start conducting your classroom from a Gestalt approach, and let your students know that you are approaching curriculum from the view that people as well as systems are more than the sum of their parts. This includes actively and collaboratively learning from your students.

Consider letting your students evaluate you and your teaching. You will truly see where they need more assistance, and you will see where you can grow and improve. As a Leader-teacher, you have a pretty good idea where you need to improve, and if you start asking your students how you can better serve them, there will be no doubt where you will need to concentrate your professional development.

Incorporating Spiritual Practices

Below are Stage-specific practices designed to do two things: they will honor and celebrate the Stage you are at, and they will prepare you for the expectations of the next Stage. While it is your goal to develop into more advanced stages, this will happen more quickly if you express understanding and gratitude for the Stage in which you currently are. Full appreciation for the wonderful person you already have become is necessary for spiritual growth.

Leader-teacher Prayer

Thank you for the peace I enjoy every day;
please guide all of us in our actions
so that peace may exist everywhere in the world.
Help me impart wisdom to my students, and
to teach them how to be citizens of the world.
Guide me as I seek to grow
in my trust of my own intuition and
my ability to discern truth.
Bless me with the ability to see potentials.
Keep me on a path of love and wisdom.

Leader-teacher Meditations

You will need to read through this entire meditation before you begin. Sit as comfortably as you can. Spend a couple of minutes with your mind blank. See what thoughts come to you. To begin your Leader-teacher meditation, close your eyes and picture a bright deep purple light in your mind.

Picture yourself sitting on a cloud. Wait patiently and see who comes to visit you. Do not concern yourself with whether this visitor is your imagination, an angel, a guide, or a deceased relative. Certainly, it is one of those!

Get out of your head and be in the mystery. Be open to what the entity brings to you in the way of a message. Perhaps he or she will speak to you; perhaps you will be shown an image or a scene; perhaps you will be given an object or a symbol. The important thing is to rely on your own intuition to determine what the message is for you.

If you are unclear, or if you are resisting what you think is an overactive imagination, you can ask this entity for clarification. You will get it. If not at that moment, then some time in a dream or in a cognitive flash during the day. You also may ask this entity your own questions in the same way, but it is wiser to let this introductory moment be a time for you to receive the message that he or she has for you. On another day, you may go to the cloud and specifically ask for this messenger, and specifically ask him or her a question.

Leader-teacher Journaling

For the next several weeks—for a time period that feels right to you—keep a log of the dreams you remember. After you record the dream, record your immediate impression of it. What do you think it means? Why would you be dreaming about this right now? If you want, you can go to a bookstore and get a book on dream symbols and dream interpretation, but you really do not have to do this. What is important is how you interpret what you have chosen to remember.

In addition to recording your dreams, take the time to record any daydreams or imaginings you have during the day. What was it that interrupted your day? What are you obsessed with? It is important to note these things and then see how they feel to you as you write them down. Do you see that you need to clear something out of your head? Have you become addicted to a thought or an emotion? Is there something that you should be tending to?

These are the questions to ask yourself when you have seen what it is that your mind focuses on when you let it wander or find it wandering. Remember that your thoughts attract like reality.

Leader-teacher Movements

Slow, disciplined movements that employ your mind are best for you in this stage. Try yoga or Pilates.

Leader-teacher Music

The Leader-teacher should listen to as much string music as possible. Some suggested artists are the following:

Toumani Diabate: New Ancient Strings.
Yo Yo Ma
Catrin Finch
Armik
Andreas Vollenweider

The Leader-teacher is summarized in the table below:

Table 6.1

View of self	Inspirational
Motivation	To live in the now
Strengths	Wise; truthful
Weaknesses	Detached; unreliable
View of others	As having the ability to guide others to transformation
View of God, spirituality	There is one God, many wells. All people are capable of direct two-way communication with God. Seeing and understanding the many faces of God is most important.
View of education	Understand the use of knowledge; evolve thought
Instructional strategies	Projects; portfolios
Classroom management	Out of understanding what is needed
Use of curriculum	Incorporate different ways of knowing
Necessary to move a stage	Understand the limits and the purpose of the material world

Stage 7

The Healer

In the beginning was only Being, One without a second. Out of himself he brought forth the cosmos And entered into everything in it. There is nothing that does not come from him. Of everything he is the inmost Self. He is the truth; he is the Self supreme. You are that . . .

—The Chandogya Upanishad

TIMOTHY

Timothy seems odd to some people—probably because he is hard to figure out. But he is very likeable. And, as do so many highly advanced souls, he seems to talk in riddles. He has more questions than answers, a story for every situation, and a countenance that makes it seem as if he really might be up to something he should not be. He is calm, happy, and has a glint in his eye.

When talking to Timothy, I have the sense that he is about to say something naughty or irreverent. At first I decided that this is because he is self-censoring and not willing to share everything with me, to instead make me figure things out for myself. Later, after reflecting on Timothy, I decide that such people appear amused with much in life because, from their perspective, life is pretty amusing. Timothy is a Healer-teacher. He is in an advanced spiritual state, therefore he easily can see the absurdity and humor in the little things that we humans tend to take so very seriously.

Timothy is a first-grade teacher—perhaps another reason people think he is odd. Even in this day and age, the male early childhood education teacher is not common. He has been an early childhood teacher for his entire career, although he has taught in several different towns in many different states as

111

he followed his nomadic wife's interests. This was fine with Timothy, because to him his career was a way to experience life and influence young people—it really did not matter to him where he was.

Timothy is married and has one son in his early thirties. He also is a teacher. Timothy's wife Melissa used to be a teacher, now she is a master gardener, and he talks admiringly about her work. "She had a brush with death, and now understands what is important to her. She knows to spend time listening to God, and she has found that in the stillness of nature she more easily does this." Timothy laughs, "Besides, this results in some great recipes made with very fresh vegetables."

I sit back and hear more about their life together, and I imagine comfort and romance. He speaks of long walks, quiet nights under the stars, slow dances to jazz music, hours in the kitchen preparing meals, and laughter around the fire. In addition to finding God, Timothy apparently has found true love, or maybe because he found God, he found true love, or maybe because he found true love . . .

In every school in which he has taught, including this current one where he has been teaching for twelve years, Timothy banters with his colleagues. They enjoy the stimulating conversations they have with him—conversations that always seem to come back to philosophical stories and life lessons imparted lovingly and free of judgment. They love how he takes their thinking to a higher level and how they are sure to learn something new about themselves when they are with him. They also adore how he does this with a wicked sense of humor.

Many people have inquired of Timothy why he works with first-graders. "Aren't you bored with them Tim? Don't you wish you could impart your knowledge and wisdom to kids who really could make a difference with what you are telling them?"

This is the type of comment Timothy is used to hearing, and his response is consistent. Because he believes in planting seeds, which at its heart is an act of faith, he tells them: "They won't always be first-graders." Because he sees all people as equals, regardless of their ages, he adds "and they are only first-graders on the outside." Because he recognizes that we do not ever fully understand our purpose on earth and have to rely on faith, he reminds them; "Maybe I'm really here to teach *you* guys!"

Timothy is the curriculum specialist for the school, and it is through this function that he primarily interacts with his colleagues. "I focus them on their goals; I help them see how they can assess whether they have achieved them; and then I brainstorm with them the various instructional strategies that will get them there."

It is clear that Timothy enjoys challenging and empowering his colleagues. "And when they least expect it," he adds, "I change the goal from an educational one to a transformational one, and then demonstrate the power of love." We both chuckle. But I push him a bit by asking how he incorporates his belief system into his teaching. How exactly does he demonstrate "the power of love"?

"I don't do any conscious incorporating," he tells me, "I just live my life, speak my truth, and act loving." I ask him if it is possible for anyone to do otherwise. He smiles "now you understand. To be contrary to that is to not live your life, but to fight your life." Timothy explains that, if you open yourself up to the universe; if you are willing to not only speak to God, but also to listen to him; if you suspend your judgment of others, and increase your acceptance of self; the integration will happen naturally.

When I ask him what exactly is integrated, he replies, "Love. It is all there is. It is the essence of everything. Once you accept that, you will see it. Once you see it, it becomes integrated into your reality. Once that happens, you are walking with God. At that point you operate within a field of bliss—a field you continuously create."

Timothy has arrived at a spiritual place that enables him to be detached from outcomes. He lives in the now. As a result, he is as content with pain as with pleasure, and with sadness as with happiness. He accepts everything as "what it is" and "meant to be." Timothy is not caught up in the things that drive the rest of us crazy. He does not play the same worries or concerns over and over again in his head. He just lives.

Because of Timothy's age—late-fifties—he is aware that this is not easy for others to understand or emulate. "I know that, even if I don't share or borrow their worries, I still need to validate the concerns of others. I need to let others know I care, even if I do not become emotionally invested in their drama. I care about their emotional and physical comfort, even though at the same time I hold the belief that all is as it should be."

Timothy tells me that one of the best ways to truly show you care is by being fully present with people—that really is all anyone wants. "They don't really expect you to solve their problems or the world's problems. They want to know that you care and that they are not facing their problems alone. None of us wants to be alone . . . really. Think about what people say when they are mad and lashing out: 'you aren't listening; you don't care; you don't understand.' You don't hear people say 'you didn't fix me; you didn't make my pain go away; you didn't solve my problem.' That is not what we look for in other human beings. We are a smart bunch and we know we have to figure things out mostly for ourselves, we just want someone to be on the journey with us."

Timothy takes my hand and looks deeply into my eyes: "Be present in all you do," he tells me. "That is all we really have, and that is the only place relationships exist."

Timothy is an attentive listener indeed, and when I talk, I feel as if I am not only the only person in the room, but also the only thing on his mind. He is right; it is a very rewarding and validating feeling. It causes me to feel more comfortable around him and more willing to share aspects of myself. It occurs to me that this may be an important component to the Healer-teacher personality. I ask Timothy what he thinks.

Timothy reminds me that healers do not heal others, rather they direct others to God's power and the power within themselves. This is a critical distinction he tells me. "People who care about you give you control, and that control is something you let a higher authority guide." Quoting Luke 17:21, Timothy states, "the Kingdom of God is within you." "Use it!" he exclaims.

Next, Timothy points out that we can seek guidance and support from others without giving away our power or taking away their ability to manifest: "Solitude, contemplation, prayer—it is all important, but we also need other people—that is why God did not give us each our own planet! We are here to experience each other and to grow from that experience. We are born alone, die alone, and find God alone—but everything else is an act of communion."

Timothy goes on to explain that this does not mean that we give others dominion over us. All of our decisions must be our own. He tells me "sometimes when people are on a spiritual quest, they are too quick to let others tell them who they are and what they need—whether this is a pastor, a psychic, or a self-help author."

Timothy makes a strong third point by explaining how we can be discerning about who we bring into our lives as helpmates: "I think a great piece of advice is Matthew 7:16 where we are told that we can tell whether a person is good or not by looking at what he produces. That tells me two things: first get to know someone well before you share yourself; and look at their life with a discerning eye to determine whether they surround themselves with goodness and produce goodness."

At this point, I ask Timothy if he thinks that quoting the Bible might get in the way of reaching out to others and gaining their trust and acceptance. "After all," I suggest, "not everyone is Christian." "Yes, yes," Timothy exclaims quickly, "you are absolutely right. I am very careful about that. There are important messages that Jesus left us—messages that can help everyone— but only if they are received. I meet people where they are, and I speak to them in the language they can hear. That is what Jesus did too. That is what parables are all about. Our God is not a small God—he speaks through many.

If I cannot find the words myself, I quote others—sometimes the Bible, sometimes the Koran, sometimes the Vedas, sometimes a poet such as Frost or Angelou or a political leader such as King or Ghandi. There is no shortage of people who have walked with God."

ARE YOU A HEALER-TEACHER?

Do you see how you are emotionally detached from outcomes? Do you see how you personally influence the lives of others? Do you understand your own connection to the divine? Are you committed to peace and justice, and to you operate from a base of love? Do you know you are here to make a difference in the spiritual lives of others? Are what others refer to as paranormal experiences a natural occurrence for you, and something you can often understand and control? If so, you are a Healer-teacher.

Healer-teachers are understandably rare, which is unfortunate, because we desperately need them now. We need them to help bring our world peace and to save the planet we seem intent upon destroying. Their ripple effect is extraordinary.

The Healer-teachers we do have would be adept in any type of teaching, but it is likely that they will find themselves in areas where they can use their healing techniques to help others with psychological or physical issues. A Healer-teachers may be attracted to special education, counseling, or healthcare. Healer-teachers are not interested in power, but they can be interested in systems changes—as was Christ. So, they may find themselves in positions of power such as those involved with policy-making but most likely they are advocates making noise at the periphery.

If you are a Healer-teacher, you operate from faith and love. You are always on a journey, not knowing where you are headed. In fact, your life journey is continuously filled with sub-journeys. Maybe you start an intellectual journey, such as taking a course at a nearby seminary, or maybe it is a physical journey, such as bicycling in Europe with no itinerary and no hotel reservations.

You are service oriented, but even when you are just having fun, you are aware of the consequences of all of your actions, and you seek to make those actions consistent with a higher good. You tend to be happy no matter what happens, and you are deeply committed to doing what you can to make the lives of others happy, from smiling at strangers to dedicating substantial time in community service.

Faith and love serve you well. Life is pleasurable and meaningful to you. You attract goodness into your life, and you bring it to others.

Life is rarely painful for you. There are two reasons for this. First, you are daily creating the life you want, which is generally pain free, and second, any pain that does come your way you accept as the aspect of life that makes pleasure recognizable and enjoyable. You allow pain, whether emotional or physical, to enter and leave, but you refuse to dwell on it or let it dwell in you. You honor it as a part of the human condition, but you dismiss it as soon as you learn a lesson from it.

Your uninterrupted connection with God keeps you as more of an observer than a participant in earthly dramas. You see that much of what distresses us in life are things we create, perceptions we choose, and reactions we indulge. You understand that life as we create it is just the projection of energy on our sense organs.

You are not fearful for your human life and physical existence. You see death as a natural transition, and that gives you enormous freedom to do what is right and what is good. You have no reason to operate from a base of fear, hatred, or scarcity. There is little temptation to do wrong, because you are motivated by love and guided by God.

Once someone reaches this Stage, there is not much danger that he or she will move permanently back to an earlier Stage. There may be times, however, that the Healer-teacher chooses to operate more from a Leader-teacher orientation only for the convenience it provides in relationships and the need to reach and teach others. But, once one experiences the ecstasy that goes along with a strong connection to the Unknowable Knower, detached contentment and the unbounded energy of stillness, one does not go back.

Your Strengths

The Healer-teacher is peaceful, and integrates his communication with God into his entire life. He literally is always in prayer.

He knows that he is in charge of his field of reality. He knows that his physical, emotional, and spiritual energies are connected to that of others, and he uses that synthesis for healing of himself, others, and the planet. Like a true son of God, he uses his connection to God and his own spirituality to harness and order energy.

He knows that in addition to having the ability to heal, he has lessons for people. He knows that he can impart to others a deeper understanding of God and how the world works. People are always better and happier in his presence and often become eager to learn why and how to create the feeling when away from him.

As Caroline Myss (1996) tells us that "your biography becomes your biology" (p. 58). Your thoughts are energy forms that enter your biological system and manifest into specific illnesses or harmony. Georgetown Medical School professor, pharmacologist, and best-selling author Dr. Candace Pert (1999) tells us that thought alone can change our bodies.

If you are a Healer-teacher you understand that the field of reality includes your body and that your body is an energy system as well as a biological system. You know that these systems are fully integrated. So, you eat right and exercise in order to tend to your biological body, and you think right in order to tend to your energy body. You keep garbage out of both systems.

Your Challenges

As a Healer-teacher, you have very few challenges on earth. Your primary concentration is on advancing your soul and your divinity. When you do have difficulties, they tend to be residual from the Leader-teacher Stage. For instance, you do not fit well in rigid hierarchical systems, or any system that is not organic.

You also have a difficult time holding on to details. After you have taken care of a situation or person, you likely will not have any reason to remember all aspects of what happened. When you are done with something, you are done. Since this is not the case with other people, you will be challenged to connect to past details while helping them move into the present.

As a human, it is not always easy for you to stay in a state of grace. You are so eager for others to find the peace and happiness that you have, that you are tempted to control them—or at least to cajole them. You have to consciously remember that your path is not their path.

The Kabbalah Zohar says that there are three parts to the soul, and the third part, the Neshamah is the divine spark, and it is activated in us when we seek righteousness and purity. The Healer-teacher has activated that divine spark and is a mystic. He has a symbiotic connection to the divine. As he seeks the divine and to do the right thing, the divine seeks him back. He is a transmitter of grace and celebrates beauty. He understands that all things are divine and all things are made of love—the essential energy of all life and matter on earth. You still can be impatient and you still need to work on unconditional love. That is the greatest challenge of humans—to understand that all matter is energy, all energy is love, and all energy can be moved and expanded.

Your Relationships

A Healer-teacher takes his spiritual practices seriously, and that is noticed by others. Colleagues, students, family, and friends turn to you for advice, and they know that this advice will contain a spiritual and philosophical dimension. That generally is what they are looking for when they come to you as the Healer-teacher. You get to know people on a deep level because they never feel that they are wasting their time or energy with you. They know you are totally present and that you truly care about them. They know that you will be honest and that your word can be trusted.

Sometimes however, people seek too much from you. They feel connected with you, and they think this means either that you can help them no matter what the problem or that there exists the basis for an ongoing relationship. They are drawn to your energy because people are hungry for true communication and the trust that can be built from that. They let their guard down, and their boundaries too. That gives you a power over them that you know they should retain for themselves. That is part of what you can teach them.

You also know that such eager people can be taken advantage of by con-artists and charlatans. It is hard for some people to tell the "prayers" from the "preyers." It is especially hard if they have not evolved their own spiritual selves to the point that they rely on their intuition and divine guidance.

You learned much of this as a Leader-teacher, but now as a Healer-teacher, you are equipped to demonstrate for people what pure love and real manifestation looks like, and you can show them their own connection to the divine. As Hildegard of Bingen realized, we are instruments of God: "the marvels of God are not brought forth from one's self. Rather, it is more like a chord, a sound that is played. The tone does not come out of the chord itself, but rather through the touch of the musician" (Fox, 2002, p. 57).

You are dedicated to peace and a personal Zen-like existence, so you attempt to heal people who indulge anger and create negativity, by redirecting them, modeling for them, imparting wisdom, and sharing your energy. However, you do not judge them. You understand that worry and fear are things people need to evolve out of. At this Stage, you are adept at not taking on their negative energy, but you still need to remember that you must have time alone to build back your strength and energy.

Your World

Schilling (1775–1854) said that matter is slumbering intelligence and that the whole universe is within man. There is a world spirit, and you have learned this. Maybe you have read and understood it; maybe you have been taught by a religious leader or spiritual guide; maybe you have had a mystical experience where you have been shown it, but you understand that we are all one—we are all made up of the same matter and substance, and we are linked through a collective unconscious.

Your view of the world is similar to that of our great prophets and mystics. "All mysticism is characterized by a passion for unity. To the mystic, true Being and Ultimate Reality are One. This can be experienced as both impersonal and personal, as Ground of Being, Ultimate Source, Perfect Goodness, Eternal Wisdom, Divine Love, God, or the Godhead. This Reality contains, yet transcends, everything there is. It is the One in whom all is lost and all is found" (King, 2001, p. 15).

Ken Wilbur (2001) describes the central mystical experience this way. "In the mystical consciousness, Reality is apprehended directly and immediately, meaning without mediation, any symbolic elaboration, any conceptualization, or any abstractions; subject and object become one in a timeless and spaceless act that is beyond any and all forms of mediation" (p. 6).

You believe that everyone is able to find answers to his or her questions by going within and listening to that still small voice. You may clearly see the path that someone should take, but you know that it is not your place to tell others what to do. You may suggest a course of action, and you may point out a path, but more likely you will find ways to help the other person discover those choices on his or her own. You are spiritually evolved, but you do not call yourself out as special, as this could make others feel deficient. The truly highly evolved soul seeks to make others feel better about themselves, not worse.

This is what makes you different from a Leader-teacher. You know that part of the growth necessary to become a Healer in one's own right is to discover what his or her path is and how best to find it, while understanding how our paths are intricately connected one to another: "Man did not weave the web of life, he is merely a strand in it. Whatever he does to the web, he does to himself" (Chief Seattle).

The Healer-teacher also is not likely to ascribe to one particular religion for he believes as did Hindu Sri Ramakrishna (1942) that there are many paths to God, but only one God:

> "God has made different religions to suit different aspirations, times and countries. All doctrines are only so many paths; but a path is by no means God Himself. Indeed, one can reach God if one follows any of the paths with wholehearted devotion. One may eat a cake with icing either straight or sidewise. It will taste sweet either way."

As a Healer-teacher, you see everyone's path as sacred and part of God. The words of Marsilio Ficino (1433–1499) capture what you would like everyone to grasp: "Know thyself, O divine lineage in mortal guise!"

Your Approach to Teaching

The Healer-teacher understands that education is reciprocal. He understands what Montaigne was pointing out when he said he does not want a teacher to think and talk alone: "I want him to listen to his pupil speaking in his turn."

As a Healer-teacher, you want to help each student discover his own divine lineage, his purpose, and his own life path. You see traditional educational disciplines as a way for a student to anchor or define his path, but you do not see it as the same as a path—just like a career is not the same as a path.

This means that you understand how important it is that a student direct his own course of study and co-teach himself. Certainly, you believe that there are certain core concepts one must know to understand how our world operates, but even in the elementary and middle-school years, you want students to contemplate what it is they need to know to be what God has put them on earth to be.

The primary foundation that you think children need is an ethical one. The Healer-teacher has an orientation very much in line with Toltec wisdom presented by Don Miguel Ruiz (1997) in The Four Agreements, and this is what your instruction should, and likely does, reflect. Ruiz urges us to be impeccable with our word, to not take anything personally, to not make assumptions, and to always do our best.

You also understand the importance of teaching children how to control their minds and instead listen to their hearts. In the words of Rumi:

That barbed wire on your path is the mind
Cut the wire and your path clearly find.
Heart trickster, soul veil and mind bind
To find the path you must put all three behind.

There are many ways for you to let students have control of their education. Make sure you continue to incorporate your successful teaching methods from the Creator- and Leader-Stages. Perhaps the easiest is to have student-led groups that discuss what they have learned and what they want to learn. Allow students to construct with each other meaning around the "facts" that you present. Start by having them explore what an answer is and where correct answers come from. What makes something correct? Who decides?

Allow your students to see how all things are interrelated. Explore the ethical nature of situations from all points of view. What is justifiable, when is it justifiable, and to whom must it be justified? When they do come up with answers, have them explore why they think this and who else thought it. If it is a scientific or mathematical fact, have the students discuss who invented it or discovered it? Why was it discovered? Who benefited from the discovery? What kind of knowledge would have to be driven underground at that point?

You do not want to be afraid to take your students on spiritual journeys as well. Give them time to sit in silence. Offer them opportunities to create art, music, and poetry as a way to tap into a different level of consciousness. Have them act out various religious and spiritual beliefs in a cultural context. And make sure that they understand the math and science behind quantum physics including what has been discovered about our ability to control our environments and the ability of an object to be in two places.

Let your students learn about (not experience) alternate realities, such as what American Indians may have felt with peyote; what Sufis experience when they whirl; what Shamans discover in a trance journey. In other words, let them explore the division, or lack thereof, between our mental and physical selves. Discuss with them why human beings desire such activities—what the purpose is.

Curriculum is evolutionary for the Healer-teacher. He builds upon and assesses what is organically imparted in the classroom by all participants. When he does rely on competencies, they are developed in cooperation with students incorporating their goals. So make sure that mastery and progress is demonstrated in student portfolios and presentations in which the student and teacher agree on the most authentic artifact and measurement.

As a Healer-teacher, you are not likely to find personal satisfaction at professional development opportunities. You do most of your work in solitude and internally. There are educational techniques that you can still learn and adopt though, so professional development is important for you, and going in person rather than doing something online, is a benefit that you give others through your presence.

Incorporating Spiritual Practices

Below are the Stage-specific practices that will honor and celebrate the Stage you are at.

Healer-teacher Prayer

> *Thank you for giving me the gift*
> *of healing hearts and minds*
> *by harnessing love's power.*
> *Help me to be a light for all those who encounter me,*
> *especially my students who so often look up to me.*
> *Guide me so that the example I set for my students*
> *shows them clearly that we are all one*
> *and bring them to understand their own divinity.*
> *Make my mistakes few,*
> *bless me with the continued ability to create what I truly need.*

Healer-teacher Meditations

You will need to read through this entire meditation before you begin. Sit as comfortably as you can. Spend a couple of minutes with your mind blank. See what thoughts come to you. To begin your Healer-teacher meditation, close your eyes and picture a bright violet light in your mind.

Think back to the words of Chief Seattle: "Man did not weave the web of life, he is merely a strand in it. Whatever he does to the web, he does to himself."

Now sit quietly and picture that web. Picture it as golden and shimmering. Find your strand in it. Look lovingly at the strand for a minute. Think about how miraculous you are. Now follow your strand and see everyone who is connected to it. Let your mind be free. Again, be in the mystery and see where you are in the entire web.

Now imagine that this is the tree of life and the strand is a branch. Where is your branch? What do you notice about your branch? What other branches are near to yours?

Healer-teacher Journaling

As a Healer-teacher, your journal can serve the function of helping you create your day and create your life. You are now adept at manifesting your intentions. Take the time to write these down. Take time also to write the miracles that happen to you—the coincidences that you know you have created.

Keeping such a journal will keep you aware and appreciative of your abilities and the gifts of the divine. You also have much that others may find helpful. Write your prayers and the messages from your meditations as well.

Healer-teacher Movements

As a Healer-teacher, it is important for you to stretch your muscles as you prepare for sitting in silence and stillness. As a Healer-teacher, you will spend more and more time meditating, praying, and contemplating. Prepare your body for this by keeping your muscles stretched and toned.

Healer-teacher Music

The Healer-teacher should listen to as much flute as possible—particularly native and Peruvian flute. Some suggested music is the following:

Ann Licater's Flute for the Soul, http://www.fluteforthesoul.com
Gheorghe Zamfir on panpipe
Robert Gass
Jean Pierre Rampal

The Healer-teacher is summarized in the table below.

Table 7.1

View of self	One with all
Motivation	To be one with God
Strengths	Peaceful; non-judgmental
Weaknesses	Incompatible with hierarchy; has trouble holding details
View of others	As aware or unaware equals
View of God, spirituality	We can be one with God. That is all that matters; that is what is most important.
View of education	Understand self in the world; a necessary game
Instructional strategies	Service-learning
Classroom management	It does not have to be managed—it is fully functioning
Use of curriculum	Connect soul to material world

Note on Case Studies

The individual case studies presented for each Stage are enhanced accounts of various experiences I have had and witnessed.

The teachers in this book are not actual persons, but rather they are composites of teachers I have had the pleasure to work with, observe, and instruct. These characters were developed to best demonstrate the particular Stages, and any substantial resemblance to actual persons is purely coincidental and an illustration of the precision of the particular Stages.

The table below shows the meaning and origin of the names used in this book.

Table 8.1

Name	Meaning	Origin
Naomi	Precious one	Hebrew/Japanese
Caroll	Champion	Celtic
Ramon	Protector	Latin
Chad	Of great love	African
Maya	Creator	Hindu
Amirah	Leader	Arabic/Muslim
Timothy	With God	Greek/Christian

References

Aquinas, T. (1952). The summa theological. In R. M. Hutchins (ed.), *Great books of the western world.* (Fathers of the English Dominican Province, trans., revised by D. J. Sullivan). London: Encyclopedia Britannica.

Aristotle (1952). Metaphysics. In R. M. Hutchins (ed.), *Great books of the western world.* (W.D. Ross, trans.). London: Encyclopedia Britannica.

Arrien, A. (1993). *The four-fold way. Walking the paths of the warrior, teacher, healer and visionary.* San Francisco: HarperCollins.

Bhagavad Gita (1993 ed.), (Sir Edwin Arnold, trans. 1899). Mineola, New York: Dover Publications.

Bonhoeffer, D. (1953, rev.ed). Letters and Papers from Prison. In J. Pelikan (ed.), *The world treasury of modern religious thought.* (pp. 462–474). Boston: Little, Brown and Company (1990).

Campbell, J. (1988). *The power of myth.* New York: Random House: Anchor Books.

Chopra, D. (1994). *The seven spiritual laws of success.* CA: Amber-Allen Publishing/ New World Library.

Collins, M. (1992). *Ordinary children, extraordinary teachers.* Charlottesville, VA: Hampton Roads Publishing.

Dalia Lama (2001). *Live in a better way. Reflections on truth, love and happiness.* [Recorded by Losang Gyalso]. [CD] New York: Sound Ideas, Simon & Schuster audio imprint.

Dana, N. F. & D. Yendol-Silva (2003). *The reflective educator's guide to classroom research: Learning to teach and teaching to learn through practitioner inquiry.* Thousand Oaks, CA: Corwin Press.

Danielson, C. (1996). *Enhancing professional practice: A framework for teaching.* Alexandria, VA: Association for Supervision and Curriculum Development.

Day, D. (1952). Confessions from the long loneliness. In J. Pelikan (ed.), *The world treasury of modern religious thought.* (pp. 285–288). Boston: Little, Brown and Company (1990).

Emerson, R. W. (1993 edition, unabridged). Self-reliance and other essays. Mineola, NY: Dover Publications.

Emerson, R. W. (1838). Divinity School Address. In J. Pelikan (ed.), *The world treasury of modern religious thought.* (pp. 244–259). Boston: Little, Brown and Company (1990).

Fennimore, T. F., & M. B. Tinzmann. (1990). *What is a thinking curriculum?* North Central Regional Education Laboratory (NCREL).

Feldman, R. (2000). *Wisdom. Daily reflections for a new era.* Winona, Minnesota: St. Mary's Press.

Fox, M. (2002). *Creativity. Where the divine and the human meet.* New York: Jeremy P. Tarcher/Putnam.

Fox, M. (2000). One river, many wells. New York: Jeremy P. Tarcher/Putnam.

Fox, M. (1995). *The reinvention of work: A new vision of livelihood for our time.* New York: Harper Collins.

Gardner, H. (1999). *Intelligence reframed. Multiple intelligences for the 21st century.* New York: Basic Books.

Gawain, S. (1978). *Creative visualization.* Berkley: Whatever Publications.

Gibran, K. (1993 edition). *Mirrors of the soul.* (Joseph Sheban, trans). Secaucus, NJ: Castle Books. [Original work published 1965].

Gospel of Sr Ramakirshna (1942) (Swami Nikhilananda, trans). New York: The Ramakrishna-Vivekananda Center.

Harvey, A. (1996). *The essential mystics. The soul's journey into truth.* San Francisco: Harper Collins.

Hopkins, D. (2002) *A teacher's guide to classroom research.* Philadelphia: Open University Press.

Jammer, M., (2002). *Einstein and religion: Physics and theology.* Princeton, New Jersey: Princeton University Press

Jax, C. (Summer, 2005). No soul left behind: paths to wisdom in American schools. *ReVision: A Journal of Consciousness and Transformation.* Washington, DC: Heldref Publications.

Jung, C. G. (1983). *The essential Jung.* (Anthony Storr, ed.). New York: MJF Books/ Fine Communications.

Jung, C. G. (1940). *The integration of the personality.* London: Routledge and Kegan Paul, Ltd.

Kierkegaard, S. (1988). *Either/or.* (H.V. Hong & E.H. Hong, ed. and Trans.). Princeton, New Jersey: Princeton University Press:

King, U. (2001). *Christian mystics. Their lives and legacies throughout the ages.* Mahwah, New Jersey: HiddenSpring.

Marzano, R. (2003). *What works in schools. Translating research into action.* Alexandria, VA: Association of Supervision and Curriculum Design.

Moffett, J. (1994). *The universal schoolhouse. Spiritual awaking through education.* San Francisco: Jossey-Bass, Inc.

Montessori, M. (1965). *Dr. Montessori's own handbook. A short guide to her ideas and materials.* New York: Schocken Books.

Miller, J. P. (2000). *Education and the soul*. Albany: State University of New York Press.

Moore, T. (1993). *Care of the soul*. New York: Harper Collins.

Myss, C. (1996). *Anatomy of the spirit: The seven stages of power and healing*. New York: Three Rivers Press.

Noddings, N. (1992). *The challenge to care in schools*. New York: Teachers College Press.

Peck, M. S. (1978). *The road less traveled. A new psychology of love, traditional values and spiritual growth*. New York: Simon & Schuster.

Pelikan, J., ed. (1990). *The world treasury of modern religious thought*. Boston: Little, Brown and Company.

Pert, C. (1999). *Molecules of emotion: The science behind mind-body medicine*. New York: Scribner.

Phan, P. (2001). *The wisdom of holy fools in postmodernity*, Theological Studies, Vol. 62, 2001.

Poll, J. & T. Smith. (2003). The spiritual self: toward a conceptualization of spiritual identity development. *Journal of Psychology and Theology*, vol. 31, issue 2.

Public Agenda.(2001) *For goodness' sake. Why so many want religion to play a greater role in American life*. (Issue report). New York.

Remen, R. N. (1996). *Kitchen table wisdom*. New York: Riverhead Books.

Roberts, E. & E. Amidon, Eds. (1991). *Earth prayers from around the world. 365 prayers, poems, and invocations for honoring the earth*. San Francisco: HarperSanFrancisco.

Ruiz, D. (1997). *The four agreeements*. San Rafael, CA: Amber-Allen Publishing.

Schweitzer, A. (1949). *Out of my life and thought*. New York: Henry Holt and Company.

Senge, P. (1990). *The fifth discipline. The art & practice of the learning organization*. New York: Currency/Doubleday.

Senge, P. et al (2000). *Schools that learn. A fifth discipline fieldbook for educators, parents, and everyone who cares about education*. New York: Doubleday.

Sinetar, M. (1998). *The mentor's spirit. Life lessons on leadership and the art of encouragement*. New York: St. Martin's Press.

Spinoza, B. (1952). Ethics. In R. M. Hutchins (ed.), *Great books of the western world*. (W.H. Harris, trans., revised by A.H. Stirling). London: Encyclopedia Britannica.

Starkman, N., P. C. Scales, & C. Roberts. (1999). *Great places to learn*. Minneapolis: Search Institute.

Steiner, R. (1994 edition). *Theosophy. An Introduction to the Spiritual Processes in Human Life and in the Cosmos* (C. E. Creeger, trans.). Great Barrington, MA: Anthroposophic Press.

Stigler, J. W. & J. Hiebert. (1999). *The teaching gap. Best ideas from the world's teachers for improving education in the classroom*. New York: The Free Press.

Swimme, B. & T. Berry. (1994). *The universe story: From the primordial flaring forth to Ecozoic Era. A celebration of the unfolding of the cosmos*. San Francisco: HarperOne.

Tagore, R. (1961). The four stages of life. In J. Pelikan (ed.), *The world treasury of modern religious thought*. (pp.149–157). Boston: Little, Brown and Company (1990).

Tillich, P. (1952). The God Above God from The Courage to Be. In J. Pelikan (ed.), *The world treasury of modern religious thought*. (pp. 300–307). Boston: Little, Brown and Company (1990).

Timar, T. & Kirp, D. (1988). *Managing education excellence*. New York: The Falmer Press.

What teachers should know and be able to do. (2002). Arlington, VA: National Board for Professional Teaching Standards.

Wilbur, K. (2001). *Quantum questions. Mystical writings of the world's greatest physicists*. Boston: Shambhala Publications, Inc.

Wiggins, G. & J. McTighe, (1998). *Understanding by design*. Alexandria, VA: Association for Supervision and Curriculum Development.

Zemelman, S., H. Daniels, & A. Hyde. (1998). *Best practice. New standards for teaching and learning in America's schools*. Portsmouth, NH: Heinemann.

Zukav, G. (1989). *The seat of the soul*. New York: Fireside.

About the Author

Christine Jax is a professor of education at Capella University, where she holds the position of Chair of Academic Innovation and Program Development.

She has worked with parents and teachers in a variety of positions including as Minnesota's Commissioner of Education and as the founder of a school for homeless children in Minneapolis. She has experience as a classroom teacher, school administrator, university professor, parent educator, teacher trainer, childcare provider, and curriculum developer.

Christine has a Ph.D. in Education Policy and Administration, an M.A. in Public Administration, and a B.A. in Child Psychology. She also has advanced training in counseling and has studied world religions.

Christine has written numerous journal, magazine, and newspaper articles, and she has given speeches, made presentations, and conducted training nationally and internationally to groups ranging in size from four to a few thousand people. She has appeared on CNN, ABC, and Discovery, and she has been quoted in *Time Magazine*, *The New York Times*, and the *Washington Post*.

She has had the pleasure of meeting Presidents Bill Clinton and George W. Bush and is proud that each has mentioned her by name in nationally televised speeches.

Her experience with children includes raising her own. Christine and her husband Jesus Castillo, a Miami Dade firefighter/paramedic, have seven children ages 27, 25, 23, 21, 14, 9, and 8.

Christine approaches life and work from a spiritual perspective that draws on her own mystical experiences and ability to connect to those with whom she works and serves. She has traveled to over fifty different countries on five continents and views cultural competency as a spiritual necessity.